THIS IS
ORIENTEERING

JIM RAND and TONY WALKER

**Published with the permission of the
British Orienteering Federation**

PELHAM BOOKS

First published in Great Britain by
PELHAM BOOKS LTD
52 Bedford Square
London WC1B 3EF
1976

ISBN 0 7207 0928 8

Printed in Great Britain by BAS Printers Limited,
Wallop, Hampshire
and bound by Dorstel Press Limited, Harlow, Essex

To
The members and officers of the British
Orienteering Federation

Contents

Illustrations

Preface

When preparing and writing this book we had in mind the requirements of three distinct groups of readers.

We hope that the early chapters in particular will be useful for both the newcomer to the sport and the casual reader, curious about the nature and fascination of orienteering and that we have been able to convey something of the atmosphere of one of the most absorbing activities yet invented by man.

Orienteering, as a sport with unique demands for a blend of mental and physical skills, defies the production of a definitive training manual but we hope that Chapters 5 and 6 will be of interest to the club orienteer who wishes to improve his technical and physical performance. We also hope that the chapters on map-making and course-planning will encourage more club orienteers to participate in, and gain more enjoyment from, these aspects of the sport.

We note that orienteering is becoming a part of the curriculum in many of our schools and colleges. We hope that the book as a whole will give background information for teachers, leaders and students, which – if used to complement practical experience – will help them relate the sport to their particular fields of work. In the final chapter we have in fact tried to address ourselves directly to the problems facing those introducing others to the sport of orienteering.

We are aware that even when the reader has read this book he will still not know the real fascination of orienteering: it is essentially a practical activity, not something that can be experienced through the pages of a book. Our intention is to persuade the reader to participate and our thesis is that orienteering is unique in the opportunities it provides, as a competitive sport, a compelling recreation and an exciting component of education today.

T.W. AND J.R.

Acknowledgements

The authors are indebted to: The British Orienteering Federation and the International Orienteering Federation for permission to reproduce material from their publications.

The friends, members and officers of the Federation, with whom we have spent many hours discussing orienteering. We value their opinions and their views have done much to shape this book but the errors and omissions are ours.

Mary and Sue, for without their tolerance and support this book would not have been possible.

CHAPTER 1

Introduction

In something less than a decade orienteering in the United Kingdom has grown from a little-known exercise for eccentric athletes and mountaineers to an established sport and recreation. It offers regular competition to some 10,000 people, increasingly finds a place on the curricula of our schools, while the staging of the world championships here in 1976 and the recognition of English as an official language of the International Orienteering Federation marks the maturity of British orienteering. In a wider view the sport has spread from its origins in Scandinavia to every continent of the world – in a recent competition in Sweden there was an entry of more than 16,000 orienteers from more than 20 different countries taking part in more than 35 classes of competition.

In the British Isles orienteering has shown its potential as perhaps the ultimate in family sports. Almost every weekend up to 3,000 people – young, old, fat, thin, fit and not so fit – run or stroll, as they will, over orienteering courses in places as far apart as the Highlands of Scotland, the New Forest and Richmond Park. In fact any reasonably wooded area a mile square may be hiding 200 orienteers, all mentally and physically absorbed, navigating their way from one red-and-white marker flag to another. Such is the nature of the sport that even when there are 200 other competitors an individual may see only a handful of them whilst completing his course.

Newspaper and magazine articles tend to depict the sport as a highly physical and competitive activity. Often they carry pictures of 'international athletes', drenched in sweat, in 'full flight' over rugged terrain. But it is important when talking of orienteering to consider the breadth of its appeal, for the highly competitive super-fit athlete is only the pinnacle of the sport; its broad base is made up of people from all walks of life, with a variety of shapes, sizes and interests. Few have any real athletic pretensions. Many regular participants find that their only other physical exertion is running for a bus. The unique nature of the sport ensures that it provides enjoyment and satisfaction for both the athlete and John Everyman – even Everyman's wife, children and dog – at the same time and in the same forest. The one factor uniting them all is a love of the countryside and the pleasures of visiting interesting and different places. From the beech woods of the Chilterns through the moorlands and forests of the North to the Highlands of Scotland, orienteers can be seen in competition with themselves as well as with their fellow competitors.

In principle the sport is rather like a 'car-less' motor rally: instead of sitting at the wheel and driving the competitor both navigates and provides the power. The course requires him to visit a number of check points, or 'controls'; at each he finds a red-and-white control flag and a punch with which to mark a card as proof of his/her visit. He navigates between controls with the help of a large-scale map and a compass. A good course offers the competitor a choice of routes between one control and the next. He must pit his wits against map and terrain and his final time will reflect how wisely he has chosen his route. He makes his decisions on the basis of his own physical capabilities and the information available to him from the map and observation of the terrain. He might decide to take a longer route around a hill rather than climb over the top, sapping valuable energy, or run on a bearing over open heathland or stick to the path in inhospitable forest. The validity of each decision will be evident in the results. Again, it would be wrong to be misled by the physical aspect; results every week defy age and the Harvard Step Test, for speed of thought is as important as speed of foot, and concentration as important as stamina.

The striking feature of the sport is the variety of its appeal. At its highest

Fig. 1
After checking the control code, stamp your card in the appropriate box

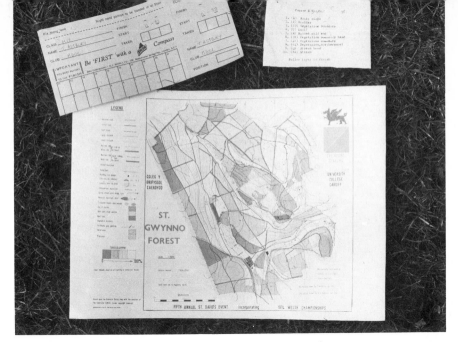

Fig. 2
*Map, control card and
description sheet*

level it is a severe test of quick thinking and athletic ability but most orienteers have their first taste of the sport less competitively – probably on a
course for 'wayfarers' (novices), where they can be content to navigate and
stroll their way around, interested only in finding all the controls and completing the course.

It is appropriate now to consider what is likely to happen when a novice
attends his first event. Although he may not be thinking of winning, we must
consider some general principles of the sport, such as competitive navigation, in order to explain its nature. Usually an orienteering competition is
won by the navigator who visits all the control sites in the prescribed order
and in the shortest time. If all competitors set off together this would involve
a procession, with everyone following the best navigator. To prevent this,
each competitor starts at staggered intervals – usually of one minute. Timekeeping is therefore a major concern for the organiser of an event; in
addition, he must distribute essential materials and information (maps,
control cards and a list of descriptions of the control sites) to each competitor and provide other basic facilities. We shall consider elsewhere the
organisation and administration of an orienteering competition (Chapter 7)
and the competitor's progress through this machinery. (Appendix A describes
in detail the sequence of activities at a typical competition, from arrival at
the venue, through preparatory steps to follow-up activities. It should be
read in conjunction with this chapter by those wishing to attend a competition for the first time.) It is sufficient at this point to briefly outline what is
likely to happen before a newcomer arrives at the start line for his first
event.

In brief, a competitor on arrival goes to the event registration, where he
books a start time on his selected course (courses are graded according to
length and difficulty), pays an entry fee and is given a map, a control card
and a description sheet.

Armed with the above, a whistle, a transparent map-case and a red pen the competitor makes his way to the start. When his start time arrives, he follows a short marked trail to the master maps, where he carefully copies the control locations on to his own map. When this is done the navigation can begin!

Figure 3 below shows a typical cross-country course. The triangle represents the position of the master maps, each single circle marks the location of a control banner and the double circle identifies the finish. The competitor's task is to select a route on the basis of the information provided by the map and then follow that route on the ground.

Fig. 3   *Typical cross-country course*

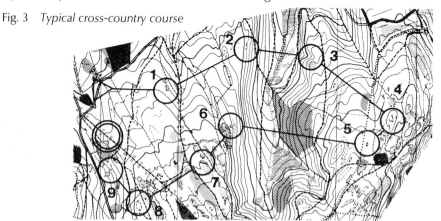

It will be obvious by now that the sport of orienteering requires a considerable degree of work, before a single competitor can set foot in the forest to find his first control. A map must be produced, courses planned, controls hung and administrative and timekeeping rôles organised.

The complexity of the organisation of an orienteering event of course varies with the nature and function of the competition: a regional or national championship obviously demands a greater degree of sophistication than a small scale club or introductory event. One of the most pleasing aspects of orienteering is the way it has grown up without the divisions, present in some other sports, between players and officials, for once a person becomes sufficiently interested in orienteering to join a club, he is both player *and* official. One week he may compete, the next he may be planning courses for others or helping with registration and making up the results ladder. Age is no obstacle to participation. The newcomer is likely to have noticed at his first event the variety in age of those taking part – from the primary-schoolboy, or girl, to the senior citizen, each participates and competes with others of broadly similar age and experience. Events are normally organised by a club and it distributes the tasks among its members. Some jobs – mapping and course-planning, for example – must be done well in advance; others will be performed on the day. At the competition venue it is not unusual to be directed to the car park by the youngest member of the club not yet out of primary school; his mother may take your entry fee and give you a start time at registration and the oldest member of the club – perhaps for several years an old age pensioner – may check your card and set you off at the start.

As the sport has grown in popularity so it has attracted members of diverse interests and ages but at its highest level it has also grown in sophistication. The top competitive orienteer is now a highly trained and extremely fit athlete – in addition to being a good navigator – but again the unique nature of orienteering as a sport means that on your first event you could meet the current national champion looking for the very same red-and-white control flag that you are searching for yourself. Such competitors obviously take their sport very seriously. They wish to avoid injury from muscles inadequately prepared for strenuous exercise and when they get to the start line they wish to commit maximum effort to their running immediately. In consequence, at the assembly point of any competition, it is common to find such competitors going through a thorough and apparently exhausting ritual of 'warm-up' exercises.

Some newcomers to the sport have arrived at the car park for their first experience of orienteering, observed the antics performed by some élite competitors in their warm-up and left without getting out of the car; having decided that anything which requires that kind of physical exertion as a preparation is decidedly 'not on'. The purpose here should be to convince the beginner that he must not be intimidated by the actions of others, for he will require a great deal of navigational experience before the extra speed and efficiency gained from a 20-minute warm-up routine will materially improve his performance, and he can console himself with the knowledge that he is not in competition with the athlete, although they may share some common controls. The élite performer's course will be between 10 and 15km and the beginner's less than one-third of this distance. If the beginner needs reassurance he should look a little more closely at the other competitors. He will find that most of the people taking part are considerably less competitive. For them the challenge and satisfaction comes from performing the navigational skills at their own speed.

No special clothing is required for orienteering. What you wear for gardening or old games kit is adequate for the first few events. The only piece of special equipment required, in addition to a whistle for safety purposes, is a compass – and even this is not essential if the newcomer selects a simple course for novices. This should require nothing more than the crudest understanding of maps for its completion.

Experienced competitors usually wear cross-country shoes and thin nylon suits (not unlike pyjamas). These are light, dry easily and offer some protection from branch and bramble. Scratches to the shins may be prevented by wearing knee-length stockings which have the front portions coated with plastic – rather like a lightweight gaiter. The purpose of this kit is to provide the competitor with adequate protection, while not cutting down his speed, but the newcomer to the sport will find little advantage in such fancy dress at his early events, rather as the novice golfer finds his brand new bag and full set of clubs more a hindrance than a help. When the beginner has gained a little experience and perhaps 'caught the bug' will be the time to think about special equipment; initial emphasis should be on old clothing and comfortable shoes, suitable both for walking or jogging over moorland or forest. The time of year, the nature of the terrain and the speed at which the competitor intends to travel should guide the selection of clothing and if the newcomer has any doubt he can always ask for advice at the event registration. Remember, however that although the rules of competition are essentially simple (see Appendix B) they do prescribe that all competitors must carry a whistle and that clothing should give full arm and leg cover.

Fig. 4
Information and directions are prominently displayed at the car park

Fig. 5
At registration you receive a map, control card and description sheet

Fig. 6
*Pre-start: await
whistle blast before
moving forward*

Fig. 7
*At the start, one
minute to go.
Then off*

Fig. 8
*Master maps, copy
down your course on
to your map*

Fig. 9
*At each control,
check the control
code and stamp
your card*

Fig. 10
Reaching the finish

Fig. 11
*Hand in your control
card*

When the newcomer has completed an event and enjoyed his first taste of competitive navigation, he will probably want details of other activities in his area with a view to joining a club. Lists of future fixtures and the names and addresses of club secretaries and event organisers are usually displayed at most orienteering events and it is possible to get general details of the sport from the national office of the British Orienteering Federation (see Appendices for address and other details), which in the U.K. is the governing body of orienteering, administers the sport through 12 autonomous regional associations and represents British orienteers on the council and committees of the International Orienteering Federation. Individuals join local clubs which affiliate to the regional associations – and hence to B.O.F. – and keep in touch with details of events, news and developments, through a bi-monthly national magazine, *The Orienteer*, and national and regional newsletters.

The sport has grown quickly in this country since the early 1960s, with its roots in Scottish forests, Lakeland moors and Surrey woodlands and yet there is a very real feeling that its development has only just begun. There remains much of the potential of this fascinating activity to be realised. We hope in the following chapters to relate the essential aspects of orienteering and speculate on its appeal as a competitive sport, community recreation and a valuable component of education.

CHAPTER 2

What is navigation?

At the centre of all navigational activities is a system of symbols or a means of communication, which conveys information through the use of plans or maps. If we are to understand what is involved in navigation it is necessary to understand the nature and function of maps.

A reader glances at the word forms on the pages of a book and has some understanding of its writer's intentions; similarly numerical symbols produce a predictable and consistent response (e.g. $2+2 = 4$). Then we can talk together and convey facts, values or emotions if we share the same spoken language. These systems of communication, subtle and sophisticated as they are, have developed through man's evolution and are one of the principal features elevating him above the animal kingdom: we are able to exchange information through the symbol systems, or languages, we share. Education promotes these skills and in school children develop a facility with each mode of communication. If communication is about conveying information, the use of maps must be one of the most sophisticated systems man has yet devised – inch for inch an Ordnance Survey map must contain and convey more information than any page of the *Oxford Dictionary* or the *Encyclopaedia Britannica*.

The above is perhaps a protracted introduction to the understanding of maps but it is an attempt to put the skills of navigation into a wider context. We regard the skills of reading and counting as relatively simple but would not dream of trying to teach someone to read using *War and Peace* as an introductory text, nor introduce the skills of numeracy through a complex form of calculus. By the same token, to consider complex Ordnance Survey maps is probably not a good way to approach the basic elements of navigation. We shall need to consider the simple skills and concepts which underpin map understanding before we can effectively use the language of navigation. Orienteering as a sport depends upon the development of the simple skills of navigation.

MAPS – PLAN, SCALE AND RELIEF

The collective term 'maps' may be confusing, for it embraces a wide and bewildering variety of forms and it is dangerous to generalise, for the nature of a map is specific to the function it is to serve. For a motoring holiday to Spain I shall need a road atlas of Europe, giving details of the major routes and towns, and covering an area of several thousand square miles, but if I ask an architect to design an extension to my house he will work from a large-scale map (plan), giving precise details of the extent of walls and fences and covering only an area large enough to show my house and those of my immediate neighbours. In both cases the 'map' is designed to serve a specific purpose and the symbols used make each sheet appropriate for specific and limited uses. However they both share the concepts of plan and scale and employ symbols to convey the information.

The first task in map understanding is to select a map – from the enormous variety available – which is appropriate for your needs. It is not vitally important that a road map show the gradients of slopes, therefore most street plans and road atlases omit this detail, but for the hill-walker this is vital information and relief is indicated by contour lines on the maps to be used. In Britain orienteers were initially obliged to use maps already available from the Ordnance Survey, but since these were multipurpose sheets they were not always ideal for the sport: they contained details which were not essential – names of hills or heights at trig. points – but often omitted small detail, such as the location of pits or recent earth-workings, which are extremely valuable for both setting and solving orienteering problems. Orienteers have therefore, since the late 1960s, been adding to the variety of maps available by producing their own and we shall discuss this in more detail in Chapter 8. However, before discussing further how maps differ, we should look a little more closely at what they have in common.

Through the symbols they employ, maps of all types are concerned with two fundamental concepts: they present a 'plan' representing locational relationships (as if the observer was directly over every point) of some area of the earth's surface and into this plan is built the concept of scale and distance relationships. Map understanding depends upon an awareness of relationships between objects, in terms of distance and location; navigational skills are built upon an understanding of these relationships. The simplest introduction to the concept of plan is probably to think of the arrangement of furniture in a room. If a single coat of paint fell evenly from the ceiling, a plan would be the pattern (Fig. 12) left on the carpet if the furniture were removed.

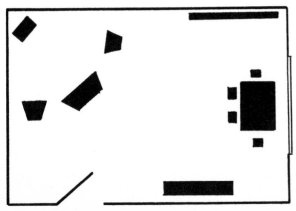

Fig. 12
Simple map of a room

21

If the concept of plan identifies the locational relationship of objects, this must be supported by an understanding of scale and the relationship of distance. The map sections in Fig. 13 show the same area, 500m square, at a variety of Ordnance Survey scales, a navigator must appreciate the relationship between distance on his map and the distance this represents on the ground. The map scales (1:25,000 and 1:10,560) explain the relationship between the map and the ground. In the first example, 1:25,000, one unit on the map represents 25,000 units on the ground. That is, each centimetre on the map is equal to 25,000cm, or 250m on the ground. By convention we use universal units of measure – metres and centimetres (or yards and inches) – but for these units to be meaningful to the navigator he must have some way of relating them to his own progress over the terrain. The orienteer therefore tends to think of distance not in terms of metres but in the number of strides (or double strides) it is likely to take him to cover a given distance.

Fig. 13
The same area at different scales:
left, 1:10,000; right, 1:25,000

A practical interpretation and understanding of maps is therefore facilitated by the ability to judge distance and relate distance represented on the map to progress through the terrain and this provides the basic concept of scale. It is one thing to recognise that one centimetre on the map, at a scale of 1:25,000, represents 250m in the terrain; it is another to be able to accurately judge the distance on the ground. It is precisely this skill in distance judgement which a practical navigator needs to develop.

If the navigator has a grasp of plan and scale then he is well on the way to an understanding of his most important tool, the map. We have observed already that some maps – street plans and road atlases – do not need to give details of height or gradient, but if the map is to be used by those travelling on foot then the relief details of the terrain will be critically important. Such maps will have a further complication, since they involve this concept of relief, that is, the symbols on the two-dimensional sheet of paper have to represent the three-dimensional reality of height gained and lost on the ground. The traditional symbol for relief is the contour line and it is probably fair to say that it is the interpretation of these lines which causes some of the greatest problems in practical navigation, for visualising the pattern represented by the plan of paths, roads, streams and other line features is relatively simple compared with the complexity of visualising the folds, mounds and undulations of the physical surface of the terrain itself.

Contour lines represent the most durable aspects of the terrain – the physical shape of the land itself – hence they convey crucial information for the orienteer but they are also the most difficult map symbols to interpret, since individually they represent an 'imaginary' line running through the whole country indicating height above a standard sea level. Each contour line is only meaningful in the context of those around it. In order to use his map the navigator must be able to visualise the physical shape represented by the contour system. Figure 14a represents a traditional attempt to show height, loss and gain, on a map with a 25ft contour interval and the other sections (Fig. 14b) indicate physical land forms and their representation by contour systems.

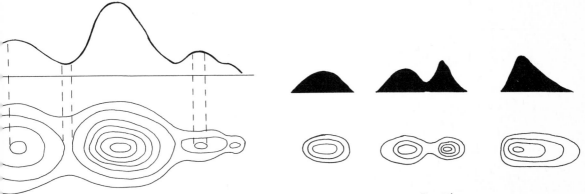

Fig. 14a
The construction of contours

Fig. 14b
*Differently shaped terrains and their
contour representation*

We have claimed that orienteering is in reality competitive practical navigation. If we ignore the competitive aspect for the moment and concentrate on the practical features, experience suggests that the only really effective way to learn to visualise the physical forms that contour systems represent is to negotiate the terrain with map in hand, read the contour lines, predict the shapes and folds they represent and then check those predictions with the ground itself. Ultimately it is only experience of negotiating terrain which facilitates and reinforces the interpretation of the symbols which represent relief. Map and compass navigation is essentially a practical activity. While it is possible to refine some skills by armchair study, there is no substitute for experience gained in the field.

ORIENTEERING MAPS

All maps convey information about plan, scale and relief by the symbols that

OPEN LAND — YELLOW

	open land
	semi-open land (scattered trees) 40% dots or lines
+10% black	rough open land e.g. moor, heath

WATER & MARSH — BLUE

Size	Feature
70% 0.2 0.4 black	lake, reservoir
0.2	river, canal uncrossable
0.5	crossable stream 2m
0.2	stream 2m wide
0.5 2.5	ditch
0.3 0.6 0.6 LT 111	uncrossable marsh
0.2 0.4 LT 70	crossable marsh wooded
+100/40% yellow LT 70	crossable marsh open
0.2 0.8 LT 68	marshy forest seasonal marsh
1.0	linear marsh
1.5	spring, source
0.3 o=2.0	well
0.3	water tank
	waterhole, small pond

LAND FORM — BROWN

Size	Feature
0.2	contour
0.5	index contour
2.5 0.5 0.2	form line
1.5 0.2	slope line
Ø 0.8 0.2	large knoll
0.2	small knoll
1.5 0.3	large depression
0.3	small depression
1.0 ∨=1.5 0.3	pit, platform
0.2 1.0	gully, difficult to cross / gully, small
0.2	steep slope 45°

VEGETATION — GREEN

Alternatives A		Alternatives B		
20% LT 23	50% LT 19	30% LT 24	+10%	
100–80% run				
50–50% slow run				
50–20% walk				
20–0% fight				

ROCK & miscellaneous — BLACK

Size	Feature
1.0 0.6 0.2	dangerous cliff (impassable)
0.4	small cliff, outcrop (no obstacle)
Ø 0.8	boulder
Ø 1.2	large boulder (if required)
	boulder field
0.6 0.3	mineshaft, cave
1.0 1.5 0.3	rocky pit
min 1.0×1.0 min 1.5×1.5	building, ruin
LT 69	built up area
2.0 L L 0.3	felled trees
1.5 1.5 2.0 0.3	cairn or boundary stone
△ 0.3	trig. point
2.0 T 0.3	fodder track
1.5 2.0 T 0.6	observation tower shooting platform
0.8	firing range
LT 88 black brown	sand
	pitted area
2.0	cemetery

COMMUNICATIONS BOUNDARIES — BLACK

Size	Feature
0.6 = 0.4	motorway
0.6 = 0.3	public/private road width 5m.
0.6	road 3–5m wide forest road
0.6	cart track
0.5 4.5 0.4	large footpath
0.5 2.5 0.2	small footpath
yellow	ride 5m wide
0.3	ride 5–10m
2.0 6.0 0.2	wide 10m wide
5.0 1.0 0.8 0.2	wall
7.0 1.0 0.2	fence
4.0 2.0 0.3 0.2	ruined wall
1.0 7.0 0.2	earthbank boundary
c.3 black	uncrossable boundary
1.0	vegetation boundary
1.0 0.3 brown	earthbank boundary
6.0 0.6 0.8	railway
0.6 0.2	power line

they employ. Orienteering maps use symbols essentially similar to those used for other maps but since they serve a specific purpose there are a number of minor amendments and special symbols. Figure 15 shows the symbols at present in use but it must be remembered that it is not possible to be entirely definitive about this since maps may be produced in one, two, three, four or five colours, depending upon the scale and budget of the competition and the complexity of the terrain.

Chapter 8 deals in detail with orienteering maps but the beginner will find it helpful at this point to consider the general categories of symbols he is likely to meet.

Black symbols on a map depict two main types of features: firstly man-made objects – roads, paths, fences, walls and the like – and then rock and miscellaneous features, such as crags, cliffs, boulders and felled trees.

Brown symbols depict the land form through the contour system and show other physical features such as knolls, depressions and steep slopes.

Blue symbols, as on most maps, depict water features – streams, lakes and marshes, for instance.

Green and yellow features, where these colours are used, represent vegetation and are important because they give the navigator vital information about this likely rate of progress through the terrain.

The 'military manual' approach to map and compass navigation has represented it as a rather remote and complex intellectual activity. One of the great contributions of orienteering has been the way it has shifted the emphasis to simple, quick and practical skills. If a skill is not simple and capable of being performed quickly, probably on the run, it will not find a place in the orienteer's repertoire. This underlines the practical nature of simple navigation, for there has not been a book written that is capable of teaching an individual to navigate (and this book is no exception). Words can, it is true, outline some of the basic skills but the efficiency of their execution will have more to do with actual experience than with the quality of the instructional book.

THE COMPASS AND ITS USES

The orienteer has two aids to navigation. The first and by far the most important is the map, for this sheet of paper contains the information that will allow him to make his route-finding decisions, to identify features of the terrain and check his progress, but he carries a second piece of equipment which offers help in this process – his compass. A common error that beginners in the sport make is to misunderstand the relationship between map and compass. They become mesmerised by the technicalities of taking bearings and, with a blind faith in the reliability of the little plastic instrument, try to negotiate all terrain in a straight line, paying little or no attention to the information offered by the map. It is important to stress to all beginners that the compass is only of assistance when the basic map-reading skills have been mastered, for without these skills the compass can be a dangerous obstacle to progress. (Group leaders and teachers would do well to consider this. It appears to be common practice to introduce navigation for orienteering, the Duke of Edinburgh Award or any form of outdoor education by considering the compass; experience clearly indicates that the map should come first.)

The value of the compass is that it is consistent and gives the navigator a fixed reference – the direction of magnetic north. In doing this, the compass provides a means of relating the map to the surface of the earth (or that area of it that the map represents), since a vital piece of information contained on every map is the direction of magnetic north. The value of the compass is that it relates the map, the navigator and the terrain to a common factor, the direction of magnetic north.

The simple cardinal points of the compass are probably well understood – most toyshops offer a simple compass in which a small magnetised needle is suspended within a housing, and a needle swings and settles to indicate magnetic north. Orienteers and most people involved in outdoor activities now use a slightly more sophisticated instrument, which combines the qualities of a compass with those of a protractor. This combination of navigational roles became known as the 'Silva System' and the development of the Silva Compass Company is closely related to the development of the sport of orienteering. A Swede, named Tillander, thought of mounting a compass on a protractor base-plate. This meant that the same instrument could fulfil the two functions of finding a bearing from a map (measuring the angle) and locating this direction on the ground. The principle was developed by the Kjellstrom brothers into the Swedish Silva System. They used the money raised by the sale of the new Silva compass to promote the sport of orienteering, first in Sweden and Scandinavia and then internationally. (Jan Kjellstrom, son of one of the original brothers, played an important part in the introduction of orienteering and its development in the U.K. in the middle 1960s. He was unfortunately killed in a car accident in 1967 and as a tribute to the man and his contribution to orienteering in this country, the British Orienteering Federation organise the 'Jan Kjellstrom Memorial Trophy' meeting every Easter. This has become one of the major competitions on the international orienteering calendar.)

The compass shown in Fig. 16 is a typical protractor type, and is, in fact, a Silva. It is made of transparent plastic and the housing in which the needle is suspended is liquid-filled. This helps to stabilise the needle and reduce the amount of swing and thus speeds up the taking of a bearing.

We may broadly categorise the uses an orienteer makes of his compass into three main groups:

1 The protractor base of the compass may be used as a measure to assist with distance judgement. The millimetre scale on the leading edge or the

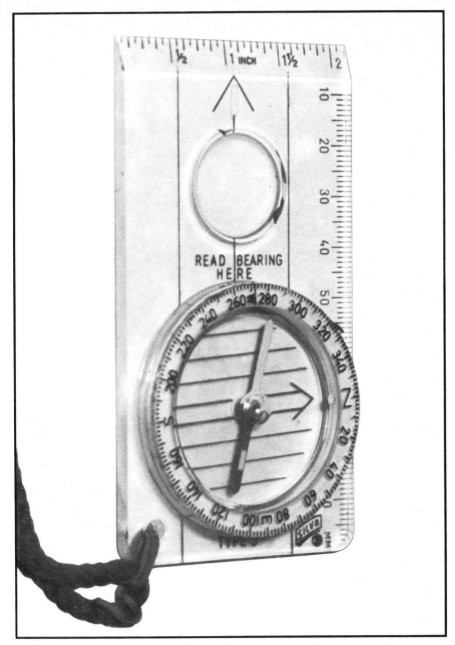

Fig. 16
A 'Silva'
Type 3 compass

side of the compass may be used to measure distance on the map, or the navigator may produce his own individual step scale and fix it to the compass (see p. 31). The purpose here is for the navigator to have some way of relating distance on the map to distance on the ground.

2   The navigator may also use his compass to 'orient' or 'set' his map. The fundamental skill in wayfinding is the ability to relate map to ground; this involves turning the map until north on the sheet (usually at the top

edge) points in the direction of magnetic north on the ground. The map can be set by identifying features in the terrain and turning the map in relation to these features but a quick and efficient way of achieving this is to align magnetic north on the map with magnetic north indicated by the compass needle (Fig. 17).

Fig. 17
The map is set; note the directions of the tracks compared with the map

3 The more sophisticated uses of the Silva compass involve the combination of its direction-finding and protractor elements, and require a little more practice than the simple uses outlined above. The navigator usually employs the compass to take a bearing from the map and uses this to establish a direction of travel. Less frequently taking a bearing from a known point and relating the bearing to the map may be necessary, in order to establish an exact location. The next chapter will discuss these uses of the compass in more detail.

CHAPTER 3

Using a map and compass

We have seen that the basic tools of navigation are the map and compass. This chapter will outline the simple skills involved in their use.

SETTING THE MAP

Perhaps the most fundamental navigational skill is that of setting the map, that is fixing the map sheet so that directions on the map correspond to directions on the ground. If an orienteer is travelling along a path which runs from east to west, then the western edge of the map should point directly in front of him. To his left, let us suppose, he can see a large valley and to the right an open field. The map should have the same directional relationship to the ground: the south of the sheet (bottom edge) should be to his left and the north of the sheet (top edge) to his right. To retain the map in the set position he must change his grip on the map every time he changes his direction on the ground in order to ensure that the features on the map correspond to the features on the land. If an orienteer keeps his map set, although he may change his direction, the map remains in the same position relative to magnetic north.

It is possible to set the map simply by identifying the physical features of the terrain and this is a skill that anyone wishing to navigate with map and compass needs to practise. There is another quick way of setting the map or checking on the set position: the top of the map sheet represents magnetic north and the red end of the compass needle also points in that direction; by aligning these two features the navigator can quickly set his map. This process is made easy on an orienteering map by a series of parallel meridian lines which indicate magnetic north (on Ordnance Survey maps a kilometre grid system is used, and the vertical north/south lines indicate what is called 'grid north'. This is variable and therefore requires a slight adjustment on the compass).

Setting an orienteering map using a compass

1 Set compass housing to north, 0/360°.

2   Place straight edge of the compass along one of the magnetic-north meridian lines, with direction-of-travel arrow pointing north.

3   Turn the map, with the compass still on it, until the red end of the compass needle points to north on the compass housing.

The map should now be set and a quick glance at the major features should confirm this. The most likely error is that the compass has been 'reversed', either because of the wrong setting at the index pointer (south instead of north) or the direction-of-travel arrow is facing south rather than north (to the bottom of the map rather than the top). It is clear at this point that a good understanding of the map provides an early check for possible compass error and again underlines the fact that the compass is only an aid to map-reading and not on its own a solution to navigational problems.

STEP SCALES AND DISTANCE JUDGEMENT

The importance of an understanding of scale has been considered. For the purpose of this section we are interested in the ways a navigator can relate his progress over the terrain with a given distance on the map. Mountaineers will already be familiar with Naismith's rule, by which they estimate their progress according to a formula allowing 20 minutes for every mile to be covered and a further 20 minutes for every 1,000ft of climbing. However, orienteers are concerned with considerably shorter distances and require a tool with a little more precision. Time is not a very realistic variable at this scale. Over the relatively short distances that he travels from known points, an orienteer checks his progress by counting his paces through the terrain and, by using the base of his compass as a measure, he is then able to relate his progress to the map. For a simple example of this let us imagine a competitor looking for a control site, a small pit, perhaps just east of a track. It is possible to establish the distance of the control site from a known point, a track junction, and let us say that this distance is 150m (on a map 7·5mm, scale 1:20,000). The navigator needs some way of judging this distance, and may only do this accurately if he knows the average length of his stride. In the situation described above if the orienteer knows that he normally requires 40 double strides to cover 100m he then needs to travel 60 double strides beyond the track junction before he sees the control to his right. To reduce the mental arithmetic the competitor might prepare a step scale for his compass which will directly relate his own stride length to the distance on the map. He will then not need to measure the map distance in millimetres, convert this to distance on the ground and then relate this to numbers of his own strides. One procedure only will be required for his unit of measure will be his own average stride length (see Fig. 18).

Judging distance by counting paces provides only an approximate measure but experienced competitors manage a remarkable degree of accuracy. To develop this skill it is first necessary for the navigator to relate his own stride length to a standard distance – usually 100m. Measure 100m

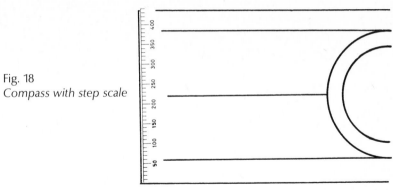

Fig. 18
Compass with step scale

over relatively level ground and then count the number of strides it takes to cover this distance. Your number of strides will of course vary depending on if you run, walk or jog but the principle remains the same: the important thing is to perform this exercise at the speed you intend to use during a competition. Repeat the process two or three times, travelling both ways over the measured distance until you are able to decide on an average number of strides per 100m. To count every stride becomes a tedious and confusing exercise and therefore most orienteers count double strides, adding one every time the left foot (right if you prefer) makes contact with the ground. Counting double strides reduces the mental effort and leaves more time to deal with the problems of navigation. Armed with this information it is a relatively simple task to prepare a strip of paper relating stride length to the map scale as seen in Fig. 18.

With a step scale, prepared in this way, the navigator has an approximate means of distance judgement but it *is* only approximate and relevant only to terrain that offers good running. In an orienteering competition the terrain varies in both surface and overall severity – from firm tracks and paths to meadow and marsh, and from flat parkland to steep forested hillside. To refine his step scale the navigator must discover how many double strides he takes to cover a measured distance over a whole variety of terrains. With experience an orienteer will be able to apply a simple addition or subtraction procedure to the basic scale to produce an amazingly versatile and accurate measure. However, as with all other navigational skills, there is no substitute for experience and no way to provide an individual with a ready-made step scale: 1:10,000, 1:15,000, 1:20,000.

TAKING AND USING BEARINGS

The third group of skills that we shall consider are those which give the navigator precision. They involve three relatively simple steps and enable him to travel from one known point to a given point or find his exact position on the map.

Let us first consider taking a bearing from an orienteering map and using it to locate a precise feature. A strange mystique seems to have grown up around the use of the compass and beginners come to expect a complex and demanding procedure – and, probably, their own failure. In fact, taking and using a bearing from an orienteering map is a straightforward process involving three simple steps, while remembering that magnetic variation must be taken into account when using Ordnance Survey maps. Let us assume we wish to travel from point *A* to point *B* (Fig. 19a).

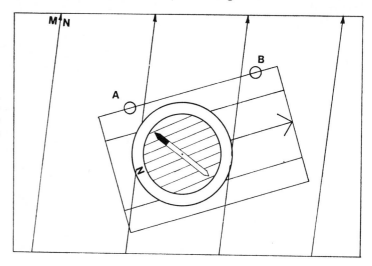

Fig. 19a
Place the edge of the compass edge between the points and in the direction of travel

Step 1

Place the straight edge of the compass base along the proposed line of travel. That is, join your known position on the map to your intended destination, and ensure that the direction-of-travel arrow points towards your objective.

Step 2

Hold the compass base-plate firmly in this position and turn the circular compass housing until the orienting lines, drawn on the base of the housing, are parallel to the magnetic-north lines on the map. It is important at this stage to check that north on the dial of the compass housing is pointing towards north on the magnetic meridian line, i.e. the top of the map (Fig. 19b). (The first two steps involve using a protractor rather than a compass.

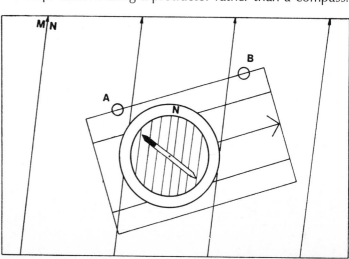

Fig. 19b
Turn the housing until the lines in the housing are parallel to the magnetic north lines on the map

All the navigator has done is measure the angle of his intended direction of travel from magnetic north. This angle can be read at the index point but since it is only of academic interest an orienteer is not concerned with the actual figures.)

Step 3
The compass may now be removed from the map and should be held horizontally in the palm of the hand, with the direction-of-travel arrow on the base-plate pointing directly ahead, i.e. at right angles to the shoulders (Fig. 19c). The compass should be held low and into the stomach so that it is possible to look directly over the dial on the compass housing and along the direction-of-travel arrow. With the compass in this position turn bodily until the magnetic-north needle is pointing to north on the compass housing.

Fig. 19c
Place the compass in the palm of your hand and turn your whole body until the needle points to the north on the housing

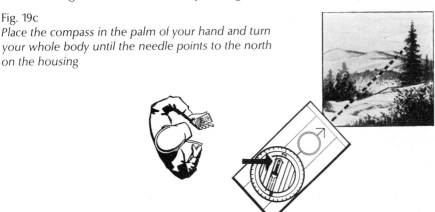

The direction-of-travel arrow now indicates the line to follow. Look up from the compass along the arrow and identify a distant object on that line – a particular tree, hill or obvious feature – and move towards it. In terrain where visibility is limited, or at night, it will be necessary to refer constantly to the compass to ensure that the correct line is being maintained. This is done by checking that the compass needle holds its position to north on the compass housing. In these circumstances it is important that the navigator is careful to move along the direction-of-travel line. Figure 20 shows that the compass retains its correct reading even when the navigator slips off this line as long as his course is roughly parallel. This error is critical in limited visibility, and a common mistake of school children when they first use a compass.

Here, in brief this time, are the steps:

1   Join the points on the map (known position and destination) with the straight edge of the compass.

2   Turn compass housing until north on the dial points to magnetic north on the map and orienting lines are parallel to magnetic meridian lines on the map.

3   Hold compass flat and into stomach, turn bodily until the magnetic needle points to north on the housing, follow the line of the direction-of-travel arrow, using a distant object as a marker.

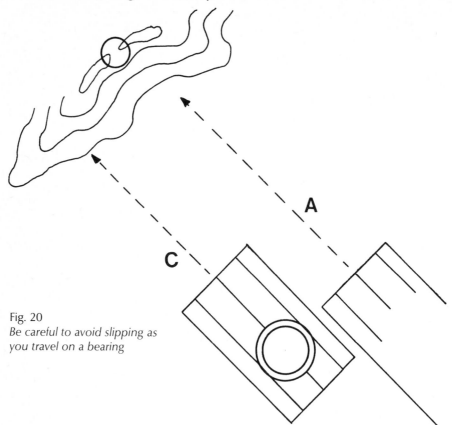

Fig. 20
Be careful to avoid slipping as you travel on a bearing

Competence will only be achieved by practice but it may be useful at this point to consider a number of the difficulties experienced by beginners. It is worth stressing the essential simplicity of the exercise. The steps are straight-forward and *care* is all that is really required – the proficiency of primary-school children at orienteering competitions every weekend is evidence of this. This is not to deny that all navigators make mistakes, especially under the competitive conditions of an orienteering event, but there is an obvious explanation for most compass error.

Step 1 is not difficult. Here, the most likely error is to reverse the compass (have the direction-of-travel arrow point away from the destination instead of towards it). This results in an error of 180°. A similar error is the result of a mistake common among beginners at Step 2. The orienting lines are turned until they are parallel with the magnetic meridian lines but with north on the compass housing facing south (the bottom) on the map. Some orienteers seek to prevent this by marking the top of their maps or printing bold red arrows on the meridian lines to avoid confusing north with south.

These first two steps are essentially simple and mistakes are easily spotted and remedied: the more serious errors are usually those involving travelling on a bearing once the compass has been taken from the map. The first difficulty can arise from the way the compass is held. Three points are important in establishing the direction of travel: first, the compass must be held on a level plane to allow the needle to swing freely; second, it must be held with the direction-of-travel arrow pointing away and at right angles to the shoulders; and third, the compass must be held in a position – close to the stomach or lower chest – where the navigator can look directly above the compass housing to align the needle. Be particularly careful to prevent compass interference from metal objects, watch bracelets, zips or buttons. Beginners also tend to twist their wrists to align the compass rather than turn their whole body.

Ideally then, the navigator, when travelling on a bearing, looks for a distant object ahead of him along his direction-of-travel line, indicated on the compass, with his line sighted in this way he may simply move towards the object. However, during a competition in forest a competitor can often see no further than 10 or 20m and following a direct line may be impossible. A single sighting is insufficient and progress can be made only by a series of sightings and constant reference to the alignment of the compass.

Perhaps, however, in struggling through tough terrain, the orienteer fails to keep to his line and loses his sighting on the feature he was using as a goal. He can tell from his compass that he is travelling parallel to his line but not if he is actually on it (see p. 34). He can, however, check his position by simply turning around and sighting on a feature he has passed and knows is on his route. This technique (Fig. 21) is known as 'taking a back bearing'. There is no need to use the arithmetic formulae of plus or minus 180° often recommended in formal texts on map-reading – the navigator simply reverses his compass, and aligns the white end of the compass needle with north on the compass housing.

Fig. 21   *Reverse bearings*

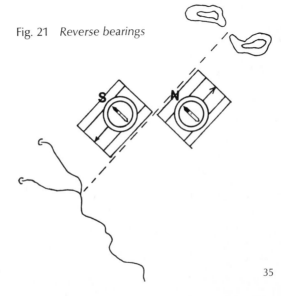

RELOCATION

It is easy to write about map and compass navigation and give the impression that success is guaranteed if a number of simple skills are mastered. Alas, the practical reality is that even the best navigator gets lost. However, experienced orienteers seem to develop a facility for relocating themselves by processing the information they gather from the physical features of the terrain and quickly relating this to the map. But for the beginner, not yet in command of the skills and experience to do this, the compass can provide a technique to accurately identify their position.

An exact position can be established by using the conventional technique of resection. This process is simplified on an orienteering map which indicates magnetic north, because there is no need to allow for magnetic variation. To carry out the procedure the orienteer must be able to identify two features on the ground and locate their position on the map. In Fig. 22 these are two hills. Having established the two features the navigator must carry out the following steps.

1   Hold the compass flat in the palm of the hand, in exactly the way described for travelling on a bearing, and turn until the direction-of-travel arrow points directly to one of the features identified for the resection.

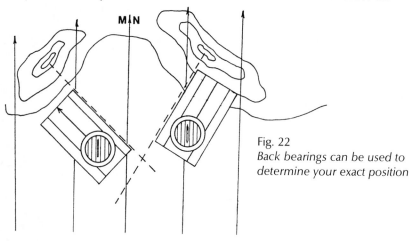

MↃN

Fig. 22
Back bearings can be used to determine your exact position

2   Hold the base of the compass in this position and turn the compass housing until north on the dial is aligned with the red end of the compass needle and the orienting lines on the base of the housing are parallel with the compass needle.

3   Place the compass on the map, with the front end of the long edge of the base plate on the feature that has been sighted. Pivot the compass base-plate around this point until the orienting lines on the base of the housing are parallel to the meridian lines on the map, with north on the housing pointing to north on the map. A line can now be drawn along the side of the compass base and the navigator's position lies on that line.

4   This procedure is then repeated for the other feature and the point of intersection of the lines indicates present position.

It is sometimes important for an orienteer to establish exact position on a long feature – perhaps a path or a stream. Since he already knows one line of the resection he can identify his precise position by sighting on one feature only. Where the line provided by this intersects with the path or stream is his position.

CONCLUSIONS

Chapters 2 and 3 have been concerned with the fundamental aspects of map and compass navigation, and the skills and concepts discussed are by no means the exclusive domain of the orienteer: they are regularly practised by the mountaineer, hill-walker or fieldworker. All navigators set out to reach a particular destination, and in their search for this objective they need to answer two fundamental questions before they can select the most appropriate route: Which direction? How far? This chapter has attempted to give an orienteer's perspective on these questions and explain the use of the essential navigational tools – the map and the compass. We would argue that efficient practical navigation depends upon a number of issues:

1   A thorough understanding of the map and the related concepts of plan, scale and relief.
2   An appreciation of the purpose and function of the compass as an *aid to* map understanding, as a measure, to set the map, and to take bearings.
3   A practical ability to judge distance on map and ground.

If these skills are mastered and combined with an ability to orient the map with the ground and judge distance, the navigator is well on the way to making the appropriate decisions about his route and answer the questions about direction and distance.

In the next chapter we shall consider more specific simple techniques, developed by the competitive orienteer.

CHAPTER 4

Beginning the sport

Chapters 2 and 3 dealt with fundamental aspects of navigation with map and compass. But progress and efficiency require practice, together with the acquisition and refinement of a number of competitive techniques. This chapter will describe a group of relatively simple skills which, if developed, will lead to more accuracy, and therefore more enjoyment of the sport.

Orienteering is essentially about wayfinding and selecting the best possible route from one control to the next. The banners marking each control should be placed so that they are easily seen from a distance of at least 20m. The skill lies in selecting the best route between controls and not in a mere treasure hunt for the banners. Course-planners will contrive to produce situations that force the competitor constantly to make decisions about his route, offer him alternatives, where he must select the route best suited to his abilities. The validity of his decisions will be judged by the time he takes to complete the course. With adrenalin in his blood and sweat in his eyes, even the most rational of men can make totally inexplicable route choices. However, the competitor does have evidence to guide his decision-making; stress may make it difficult for him to interpret the guidance that it offers but he has valuable information both from his map and his observation of the terrain. The test is how efficiently the individual acts upon the information he has, to select *his* best possible route.

We have seen that a navigator needs to answer two basic questions: Which direction? How far? But it is not that simple. It is not always possible to travel in a straight line and this may anyway not necessarily be the fastest route. An orienteer needs to consider a number of factors before deciding whether to go straight, or to seek a longer alternative.

ROUTE CHOICE

The surface, vegetation and relief of the terrain are the first important variables to be considered in route choice. In competition an orienteer is seldom offered a firm, smooth and flat direct route between one control and the next.

If the navigator draws a straight line on his map, joining the two controls, he can then decide whether such a route is possible. It may cross a deep river, climb dangerous crags, invade private property or cultivated land. Any of these features will oblige him to consider an alternative. Such a line on the map will also indicate how 'physical' the direct route is likely to be and to what extent it will require unnecessary effort – height gained, for example, that will not be maintained later on.

Each competitor varies in the way he reacts to the demands of the course and with experience learns to judge where he is likely to perform most efficiently. He will be concerned with the comparative speeds of the routes open to him – a fit track athlete might choose a route on the flat even if it involves a greater distance, as long as he considers there is the opportunity to use his basic speed. A competitor less sure of his speed might prefer to save distance and select a more direct route, even if it involves difficulties such as a climb or thick forest.

In the example (Fig. 23) three routes appear to be possible between controls 1 and 2:

a   Direct line – requires 200ft of climb.
b   Southern route – longer than a but requires only 125ft of climb.
c   Northern route – longer than both but no climb.

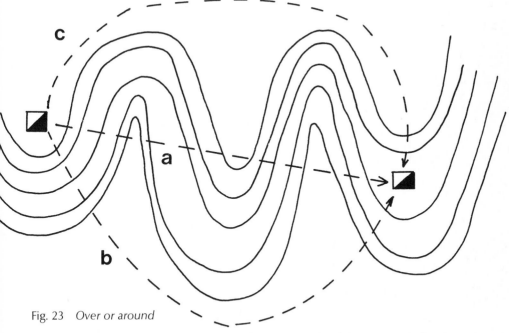

Fig. 23   *Over or around*

It would not do to oversimplify the factors involved in route choice but conservation of energy is a critical concern for orienteers and unproductive climbing is likely to very quickly sap reserves of stamina and strength. An experienced competitor will climb only when he is sure that such a route is the fastest line to the next control. (Some climbing is of course inevitable. If I stand on the floor of a valley and the next control is 200ft above me on the hillside, there is no way I can avoid the climb.)

In Fig. 23 the direct route would almost certainly be ruled out, for 200ft of climbing is likely to provide a slow route for any competitor. The southern and northern routes require closer consideration. To go south requires a climb of 125ft but this could be worthwhile if it saves a considerable running distance – especially if the competitor is not sure of his basic speed. One authority (J. Disley, 1967, p. 72) suggests that it might be possible to apply a formula to this kind of problem: 'For the detour to be profitable it must be less than the direct distance plus 100m for every 25ft climbed.' The formula, of course, depends on the fitness and ability of the individual but experience in applying it, with groups of physical education students suggests that it is not over generous in allowance for height climbed. If we were to apply such a formula to the example above, the direct line, a, with a climb of more than 200ft, would only be the quickest if it were 800m shorter than the northern route, c, which requires no climbing, or 400m shorter than the southern route with only 125ft of height to gain.

In the route-choice example we have discussed it was assumed that the surface and vegetation of the terrain is broadly consistent. We had to do this because the map gives no other information. Course-planners and mappers endeavour to produce a fair competition and strive for this by giving as much information as possible, upon which to base a route choice. Let us assume that the terrain, in the above example, is not broadly similar and the northern route takes the competitor through dense forest. If this information is not available from the map the competitor may choose this route and be disadvantaged, for the southern route may provide another competitor with free, open forest to speed through. One of the greatest advances in mapping for orienteering has involved the use of 'penetration screens' – the mappers' attempt to indicate the likely rate of progress a navigator can expect through particular terrain. For example:

Route choice will require the competitor to make decisions upon the comparative speeds of various routes, taking into account not only the 'physical' aspect of height to climb but also surface and vegetation of the terrain on each potential route. We have already discussed the need to develop a facility to judge distance by step-counting over a wide range of conditions.

It is also important for the orienteer to be able to judge comparative speed over a variety of terrains. Fastest progress is likely to be made on firm paths or tracks; 'brashing' lines or extraction lanes through the forest are likely to be slower – perhaps 'path time' plus 30 per cent – while heathland and open forest might require path time plus 100–150 percent. Thick forest can take up to five times as long to cover a given distance compared with a path. Season and weather influence the difficulty of the terrain – heavy rain can turn speedy firm footpaths into formidable obstacles of churned-up mud and clay, and open heathland, comfortably crossable at full speed in February, can become an impossible wrestle with head-high bracken and heather a few months later.

A navigator's knowledge of the 'runability' variable of the terrain can be gained only by experience. Later we shall discuss ways of developing a number of skills to improve efficiency of running through a variety of conditions. In the meantime the competitor must develop and refine his own terrain/speed ratio to apply to his decision-making.

Mappers make every effort to be consistent in use of symbols but inevitably some are hardier souls than others. The forest one mapper regards as 'walk' may become 'fight' on another's drawing-board. There can, of course, be no rigid objective scale. Consequently, an experienced orienteer will tend to play safe on the first couple of controls until he 'gets into' the map and becomes able to judge the terrain. His later decisions on route choice will be informed by early observation of the 'fit' of the map to the terrain.

THUMBING THE MAP

Orienteering is concerned with making decisions about alternative routes. The decisions are made by consulting the map and we have already discussed the importance of keeping it set or oriented, so that it can easily be related to the ground. Vital seconds may be lost each time the map is consulted if the whole sheet has to be scanned to determine the navigator's present position. This could mean several minutes wasted over the whole competition. The map may be oriented as described before but it is seldom necessary to have the whole sheet on view at any particular time. It can be folded and carried comfortably in one hand, with only the relevant terrain on view and the thumb of the carrying hand can be used to pin-point present position. Some competitors even mark a red arrow on their thumb with a felt-tip pen or adhesive tape in order to pin-point their position on the map and focus the eyes quickly on the appropriate area. This is a great aid to reading the map on the move – the ideal strived for by all competitive orienteers. With experience of reading the map on the run, if the sheet is kept in the set position, the thumb can be moved to monitor progress. This helps one consult the map and ensures a constant check on the route and an early warning of error.

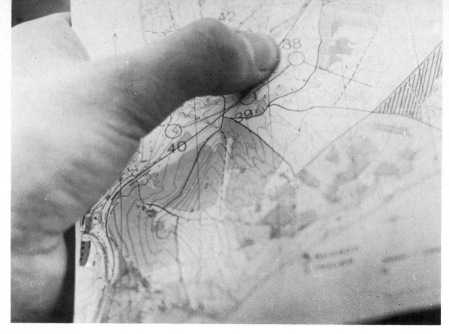

Fig. 24
Thumbing the map

SIMPLE SKILLS

While many experienced competitors develop an amazing degree of accuracy in taking and using bearings, the technique remains a chancy business over a long distance or in dense forest. Competition has produced a number of techniques which can be regarded as 'safety nets'. The importance of these safety techniques is that they can prevent a number of small errors accumulating into a total navigational disaster. The beginner is therefore well advised to practise these skills.

Aiming off

Perhaps the most common of such techniques is that of aiming off, and it stems from the assumption that there is likely to be some degree of error when a competitor tries to use a precise bearing. Let us assume that the competitor is navigating to a control point on a large or long feature. It is probably better for him to aim slightly to one side of the exact location, for when he finds the feature he can be sure which direction to turn in order to find the control (Fig. 25). If he had aimed directly at the control, made a slight error and found the feature – but not the banner – he would not know whether to turn right or left. There is also the consideration of speed of progress: it takes longer to travel on a 'fine' or precise bearing directly to the control than assume an error and run on a less precise bearing to one side – the target

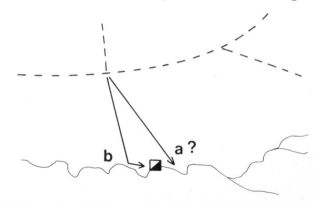

Fig. 25
Aiming off

is larger if nothing else. In the diagram, if the competitor elects to travel on a direct bearing and misses the control banner, when he finds the stream he must waste valuable time trying to decide whether he should turn right or left. It would be more efficient for the navigator to run on a less precise bearing slightly to the right of the control, then when he finds the stream he knows the banner is to his left.

Attack points

The skill of aiming off is used in a number of ways and is often combined with another fundamental technique employing the principle of an attack point (Fig. 26). While it may be possible to use a compass bearing with some accuracy over a short distance its range is limited unless the competitor is prepared to travel very slowly. He may instead prefer to run on a rough bearing to an obvious feature, identify a known point and attack the control precisely over a much shorter distance. Further refinements of 'fine' and 'coarse' orienteering will be discussed later. At this stage we shall consider the simple principle of attack points.

Fig. 26
Attack points

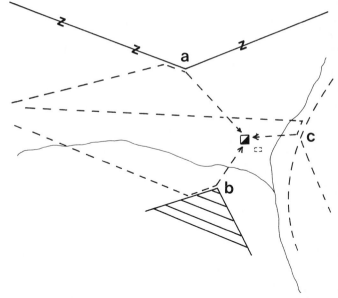

If an attack point is to be valuable it will:

1   Be an obvious feature, which is easily found. There is no point in spending time looking for an attack point which is more difficult to find than the control itself. Ideally attack points will be situated on long or large features.

2   Be relatively close to the control. In competition few orienteers are accurate using a bearing over 150m in thick forest – even with only a 10 per cent error this could result in the control banner being missed. Beginners will require attack points much closer to the control.

3   Ideally be in a position in front of the flag. This reduces the amount of unnecessary running, but a position to the side is acceptable as long as this does not involve too much additional distance. Failing this, it may still be useful even if beyond the control.

Collecting features

In the consideration of aiming off the crucial feature was the stream which ensured that the navigator could not seriously overshoot the control. Orienteers make great use of such line or linear features in their navigation. Any long or large feature on the ground which cannot easily be missed may be used by the competitor as a 'collector' or 'collecting' feature – this is really a catching device to prevent overrunning the control (Fig. 27). Fences, tracks, walls, streams or long relief features, valleys and spurs are frequently used for this purpose. Such features are particularly important when situated close to a control site and one of the first things a competitor will establish, when planning his route between controls, is which route will provide the best collecting feature. If there is a large or linear feature immediately before the control it may be possible to run quickly – without a great deal of precise navigation – to the feature, identify an attack point and locate the control by pacing on a short accurate bearing. A similar feature behind the control will tell you if you have gone too far and the control can then be approached from a new attack point.

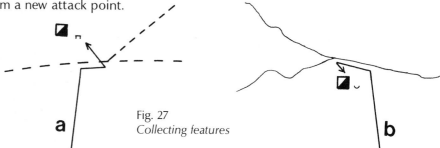

a

Fig. 27
Collecting features

b

Handrail features

Competitive orienteering of course puts a premium on time. Every consultation of the map costs valuable seconds and experienced competitors develop a number of techniques to structure and organise their study of the map and ease their progress. One way of reducing references to the map between controls is for the competitor to identify features that might guide him towards his objective. Once such features are identified progress can be both safe and swift. To negotiate complex terrain accurately is difficult and checks will need to be made to ensure that the correct course is being maintained. This becomes both a mental and physical strain. If the route of an orienteering competition were marked with streamers so that competitors had simply to follow them, élite men performers would probably run a 10–15km course at an average of about 4 minutes per km, but when the runner has also to navigate, the time required to cover the same distance might be almost doubled. The navigator needs this extra time to make his route choices and check his progress. Anything that frees him of some of these problems increases his speed. Although longer, a faster route might offer the competitor certain progress towards his objective along a line feature (Fig. 28). Such features as streams, fences, and paths may be used by the navigator as 'handrails' – when they are situated *along* his route. He can follow them at maximum speed and without constantly checking progress. There may be a further advantage in their use, for although no path is marked on the map, walls, fences and streams are among the favourite routes of animals, foresters and other users of the countryside and are often accompanied by small tracks. The handrail may therefore not only provide a safer and faster route but also be physically less demanding than a direct line through the forest.

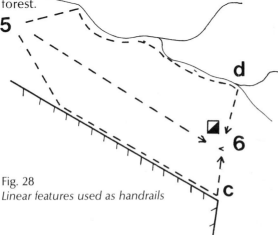

Fig. 28
Linear features used as handrails

From control to control

It might be valuable at this stage to categorise what actually happens when an orienteer navigates between one control and the next. Before we do this, a warning is appropriate: it is dangerous to separate elements of a skill and consider them in isolation. Competitive orienteering, in common with most other physical and mental skills is more than a series of isolated 'phases'. Essentially it is a single process and requires a good deal of practice, as well as analysis, before it can be done efficiently.

We may, however, with this in mind, identify three likely phases as an orienteer makes his way from one control to the next. In the first phase, the competitor must process the information available from the map, weigh the alternatives and, on the basis of his experience and observation of the terrain around him, make a choice of routes. There will probably be two phases in the execution of this route. The competitor moves quickly to a point near the control site. This will probably require 'rough' navigation and speed is the essence. From this attack point the third phase of the process allows the competitor to attack the control precisely, using an accurate compass bearing and distance judgement by step-counting.

Phase 1: route choice
The competitor must identify:

1 Location of next control and its description.

2 Possible attack points.

3 Alternative routes and detour problems – round or over? Long but easy or short but hard?

4 Useful linear features such as collectors or handrails.

The competitor must then apply his experience, observation of the terrain, and interpretation of the map to the above issues and select the route he feels will best suit his abilities.

Phase 2: navigation to the attack point
The likely first part of practical navigation involves the competitor moving quickly to an attack point close to the control site. Emphasis is on speed and simplicity. Efficient performance depends on:

1 Efficiency in Phase 1.

2 Presence of collecting features.

3 Presence of handrails.

4 Identification of good attack point.

5 Good distance judgement.

Phase 3: attacking the control
The final phase demands accuracy if the competitor is to locate the control site. This is probably the phase most likely to cost the beginner time in 'hopefully' searching for the control rather than positively 'attacking' it. Efficiency demands accuracy and:

1 Precise attack point.

2 Accurate bearing from attack point to control.

3 Accurate estimate of distance from attack point to control on map and accurate judgement of distance by pace-counting.

4 Careful travel on bearing.

We shall consider many of these skills in more detail later.

CHAPTER 5

Competitive orienteering 1: physical training

Orienteering is the skill of navigation at speed and it follows therefore that, given a well-planned course, the competitor who is deficient in either speed (physical fitness) or navigation (route choice, map-reading and compass work) is unlikely to finish high in the results. If success is to be achieved it is vital that the correct balance of speed and navigation is struck. To be either a good navigator or a fast athlete alone is not enough.

The next two chapters, relating to competitive orienteering seek to help the competitor who has mastered the basic skills to improve his technical and physical performance. We shall consider the following aspects: physical training for orienteering, navigational training, producing a training programme, preparing for a competition and finally the race itself.

In order to orienteer competitively it is essential that basic fitness is achieved, firstly in order to maintain a consistent speed throughout the race but also to avoid the navigational errors which occur when the body is fatigued. Often, towards the end of the race, the unfit competitor enters into a cycle of mistakes caused by fatigue. His tiredness leads him to a wrong route choice, he becomes more tired and makes more mistakes. This can even happen near the beginning of the race if little or no warm-up is done.

In orienteering there are five physical qualifications for success:

1 Ability to maintain good speed.
2 Endurance.
3 Terrain technique.
4 Strength.
5 All-round condition.

All of these must be looked at and trained for and this will mean time and effort, but it is vital that whatever training you do must be enjoyable. To be a top orienteer takes many years of continuous training and competitive experience, efforts difficult to maintain if not enjoyable. Occasionally short-term sacrifices may need to be made for long-term enjoyment but these must be kept in proportion to the aims.

The orienteer is more concerned with running at a steady speed than at being able to produce a fast sprint to the master map or from the last control to the finish. It is essential therefore that the orienteer makes the most efficient use of the oxygen he has available and indeed trains his body to accommodate more oxygen. This state of running is described as aerobic.

The opposite state, anaerobic, is reached when the competitor is in a state of oxygen debt, particularly when running hard up a hill or at pro-longed high speed. In this situation, because of the lack of oxygen, the body cannot efficiently dispose of the waste material created – hence the 'heavy leg' feeling. In an anaerobic state all the available oxygen is being used for the physical processes and the brain cannot perform the necessary navigational processes as efficiently as is desired. There are ways of training the body to cope with this but for the average competitive orienteer the efforts of training would be best channelled into aerobic training to achieve a steady state.

ENDURANCE

In order to improve and develop aerobic endurance several types of training can be used.

Long, slow, distance (or LSD as it is sometimes known) improves the oxygen-uptake capacity of the muscles and so resist fatigue. Of course 'long' and 'slow' are relative terms but training should be built up until you can run for an hour continuously. Only at this stage should speed be increased but never to the point at which you enter into a state of oxygen debt. However, periods of fast or steady running increase the oxygen-uptake capacity of the circulatory system, the capacity of the heart and the oxygen supply available to the muscles.

Interval running can have a dual effect of aerobic and anaerobic training but, providing sufficient rest intervals are allowed between good pace run-ning, the anaerobic state should not be reached. Run 200–300m at a reasonable pace and then jog back to the start, repeating the exercise after a short rest. This should be done at least ten times and, as training progresses, increased to 20. At this stage, rest periods can be gradually reduced – but remember not to reach an oxygen-debt state.

Finally let us consider *fartlek*, a Swedish word meaning 'speed play'. This form of training, if carried out in the pleasant surroundings of a nearby common or woodland, can be most beneficial for orienteering. An hour to an hour and half is spent alternating between steady running, fast sprints, jogging, hill running, walking, striding etc. – say, for example, 1,000m jog, 100m striding, 500m steady running, 50m sprinting, 200m slowing down, walk – and so on.

STRENGTH

During an orienteering competition, various types of terrain are encountered but inevitably you will come across hills, marshes and muddy paths and it is on these occasions your strength will be tested. The frequency of their occurrence depends on where you live and where you compete.

The best way of developing strength for orienteering is to run up a 200ft hill several times or run half an hour in marshes. If these are not available, keep an eye open for alternatives – for instance, several flights of stairs, sand-dunes, shallow water at low tide, horse rides. The list is endless if you are prepared to look and compromise.

SUPPLENESS AND MOBILITY

The ability to cope with low branches, brashings, undergrowth, fences, ditches, streams and other obstacles can have a dramatic effect on the time it takes you to cover a course.

Strength, suppleness and terrain technique will help you but there is no value in improving one to the detriment of the others – increased suppleness is of no use unless you have the strength to utilise it to the full.

There are many exercises which can be undertaken but it is important that they are carried out regularly – say each morning or evening. At first there is bound to be some pain but do not alter the exercise merely to relieve the pain. Just perform the movement gently and do not use force. A reasonable selection is:

For the spine
1   Lie on the back with hands flat on the floor at the side of the body. Push the chin to the chest; keep it there and roll forward until the head is between the knees. Lie down, again keeping the chin tucked in, and put the back down gradually until shoulders and head reach the floor. Repeat five times. Eventually you will be able to do this without bending your legs.
2   Sit on the floor with the legs as wide apart as possible, hands flat on the floor between the legs. Move the fingers away from the body, keeping the legs straight. Repeat six times.
3   Crouch, feet together, hands flat on the floor outside the feet, head beside the knees. Gently straighten the knees, putting the hands flat on the floor as soon as possible; keep the palms flat on the floor. Repeat three times.

For the hips
4   Stand with the feet together and hands to the side. Raise one leg back-wards, straight, as far as possible. Do not lean forward. Repeat three times with each leg.
5   Lie on the stomach, hands palms down under the shoulders. Raise one leg backwards as far as possible. Repeat three times with each leg.

6 Stand upright, feet together, arms at the sides. Lift up the right knee as high as possible; do not lean forward. Repeat three times with each leg.

For the ankles
1 Stand upright. Rise high onto one set of toes, keeping the other foot flat; as the raised foot is lowered the other is raised. Repeat ten times for each foot.
2 Sit on the floor, legs out straight and big toes together. Press the big toes to the ground but keep the legs straight. Repeat six times.
3 Sit on the floor, the right leg crossed over the left. Take hold of the right foot and take it through a full range of movement. Repeat twice for each foot.

TERRAIN TECHNIQUE

Terrain technique is often the most important aspect of the physical side of orienteering but all too often it is totally neglected by the average competitor. The basic fitness resulting from suitable training can usually be acquired after miles of road plodding but all training should, if possible, be carried out in similar terrain to that of competitions – after all practice on pavements only makes you good at street orienteering! Nobody lives far from suitable terrain. Even in the centre of London the parks and open spaces can be put to good use. The distance from home to the terrain can be used for warm-up and exercises, leaving the real work to be done in the right place.

Most top British orienteers can outrun a Scandinavian on the track but as soon as the smooth surface is abandoned the British are left floundering in their wake, at the same time expending twice as much energy. They lack terrain technique.

Once on the course itself, large obstacles are easily avoided by good navigation so fallen trees, undergrowth, boulders, walls and streams cause the greatest hindrance. Top orienteers, however, receive relatively few scratches and cuts whilst lesser folk regularly return with torn clothing. Technique is a matter of gently bypassing the local obstacles rather than smashing forward with your head down. Hands can be used to push branches aside and in time there is less need to keep the eyes glued to the ground – experience makes for sure-footedness. The eyes should survey the terrain 15–20ft ahead for obstacles. Your training and practice will have given you suppleness related to strength and a much better sense of balance.

Different features require different techniques. Deep marshes and undergrowth necessitate a high knee lift and in wet marshes short, gentle steps are best. The tussocks can be used as firm footing and to look ahead is really useful. The inexperienced jump and stumble, whilst others appear to 'float' across.

On hills it is generally easier to climb gradually, maintaining a run, but once you are reduced to a walk choose the steepest route. Here you can utilise your hands and arms and so divert some of the effort from the legs. Coming down is different – let gravity take you; don't hold back – this is more tiring to the legs than climbing. However, this technique does require confidence gained through practice but the time saved can be immense. Keeping the arms high for balance will also help as will coming down in a 'slalom' manner, thus avoiding excessive speed.

Knowledge and understanding of the forest can often be of great assist- For example, in Britain trees are often planted in lines so it is much easier to run down a line than try to cut diagonally through.

TRAINING PROGRAMMES

For many orienteers the season is continuous. Although domestic competition is limited during the months of July and August many journey overseas for major events – for instance to the Swedish and Swiss five-day events. It is important, however, that some rest is taken from intensive competition and training should be arranged so that effort alternates with relaxation. This applies as much to each individual training session as to periods of months and years.

The basic principle of any training programme is that the volume of training should be increased gradually over a period of time. This build-up may last for many years and starts with general basic training to provide the necessary fitness to enable a competitor to run throughout the competition. It then progresses to more intensive training to help cope with particular situations – hills, marshes, undergrowth – and finally there is training specifically geared to certain competitions or periods of maximum performance.

When compiling a training programme several factors have to be taken into account. What you are training for? For what length or peak of season, duration of event or general terrain type? What is your temperament, strength, stamina, age? How much time is available for training? What are your personal aims? Do you want to reach gold standard, be a G.B. team member or even a world champion?

A general training programme aiming at a good level of fitness for most of the season and reaching a peak in the period March to June is as follows:

July and August
Basically a rest period. One long run each week of at least $1\frac{1}{2}$ hours. Any competitions during this period should be used as part of the training programme. In addition there should be one or two steady half-hour runs.

August to December
A period for building strength and endurance. Continue with the long-distance running but step it up to twice a week. Also hill and *fartlek* sessions.

December to March

Sufficient stamina should have been developed by now and more effort is put into acquiring speed. Two *fartlek* sessions, interval running, hills and one long, slow session.

March to June

A period of intense competition. Training is eased before an event but not neglected. Continue with one long, slow distance session and *fartlek* but resist the temptation to do hard speed sessions.

A typical December to March weekly programme might look as follows:

Sunday   – competition or long, slow distance work.
Monday   – *fartlek* session including light jogging (total of 6 or 7 miles).
Tuesday   – long, slow distance work (at least 60 minutes).
Wednesday – interval work.
Thursday   – long slow distance work.
Friday   – *fartlek* session including hill work.
Saturday   – cross-country race or steady pace run of 30–40 minutes.

A schedule like the above would produce the necessary endurance and strength and then maintain a plateau of fitness from April to August, thus catering for the needs of most competitive orienteers.

TRAINING FOR BEGINNERS

For many orienteers, to embark on schedules such as the above would destroy their enthusiasm for the sport. Indeed if it were necessary they would soon look for some other form of activity. One of the charms of orienteering is that it caters for all ages, types and attitudes and yet in different ways still presents a challenge.

A large number of people come to the sport never intending to do more than break into an occasional jog – and then usually because gravity lends a helping hand – develop an urge to be more competitive. It is for these that what follows is intended.

Perhaps the hardest task for such people is to actually go out of the house with the sole purpose of exercise in mind. The ridicule of neighbours, doubts of your own ability and lack of time are the main problems. Start by walking a little more. For example, walk, don't ride up the escalators, use the steps not the lift, get off the bus one stop and the train one station earlier. Gradually your fitness will improve. Crash courses in dieting and exercise never did anyone any good and they are certainly not enjoyable. With a little self-control much more can be achieved.

Eventually, the time will come when to don a tracksuit for 15–20 minutes of jogging is easy and enjoyable. Don't rush though; once or twice a week is sufficient. As time passes don't increase the number of occasions but try to go a little further or a little faster. A simple measure of improvement is to run out on a set route for 15 minutes and then return. As your fitness progresses, so you will get a little further. If you can persuade a friend to come with you, so much the better. Or take the dog: he will appreciate the opportunity to run rather than pull!

For many people this type of training will often mean using streets – never as enjoyable as a run in the local park. So vary your routes and even the days. A regular commitment only breeds boredom.

Or course your age will influence your training programme but providing you feel you are working within yourself no harm can be done. It is sudden exertion which can cause damage – even top athletes go through a long warm-up session prior to a race.

Remember you must enjoy your training. As soon as you feel that enjoyment is slipping, take a rest or change your schedule.

CHAPTER 6

Competitive orienteering 2: navigation and racing

NAVIGATION AND TRAINING

Earlier chapters have looked at the essentials of basic navigation – attack points, collecting features, handrails, aiming off etc. This section goes on from these initial requirements and relates them to competitive orienteering.

The type of terrain that the competition is taking place over is the major factor influencing the orienteering techniques to be used. An area with large physical features – hills, marshes, crags – necessitates good route choice if the competitor's energy is not to be sapped within minutes of the start. Flat terrain with many small features – ditches, paths, boulders – requires good map-reading ability, together with accurate use of the compass and pace-counting. Obviously terrain which is a combination of both will test all an orienteer's skills most of the time (Fig. 29).

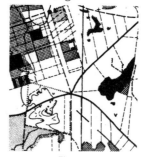

Fig. 29
(a) rugged, (b) flat, (c) varied terrain

ROUGH AND FINE MAP

In its simplest form map-reading can be divided into two distinct parts – rough map-reading and fine map-reading. In the former the navigator relies on large physical features – roads, hills, paths, streams – to act as collectors. In the example (Fig. 30) all the minor features between A and B can be ignored, since the forest road will act as a barrier to further progress. Once on the road the ride beyond can be used in a similar manner. It is only when there are no more of these prominent features between the orienteer and his objective that he must resort to fine orienteering (C to D), going more

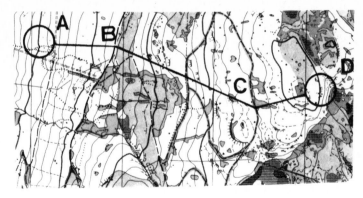

Fig. 30
Rough and fine map

slowly and mentally ticking off each feature. Possibly he may move on a precise bearing and count steps (Fig. 30).

ROUGH AND FINE COMPASS

Similar conditions of rough and fine can be used with the compass. In navigating to the forest road in the example (Fig. 31), providing you run in an approximate easterly direction, the road *must* be reached. The direction of the road on arrival determines at which side of the bend you have aimed. Much the same is true in the case of the hill, but from the hill summit a precise bearing must be followed and pace-counting employed if the correct boulder is to be located. In this instance a combination of fine map-reading and fine compass can be used.

If the leg is short and the collecting feature (Fig. 31) large it is possible to 'run on the needle' for, knowing approximately where north is, a direction of south, east or west can be run without further reference to the compass. This technique can also be used with the sun as an approximate guide and can save valuable seconds.

Fig. 31
Rough compass followed by fine orienteering

ROUTE-PLANNING

In typical British terrain this is usually more important than any other technique. Experience is essential if the correct decisions are to be made. Invariably there is a quickest route but seldom is it the safest and the competitor must also strive to achieve the right balance of speed and accuracy.

When making a route choice it is generally best to work back from the control point to your present position. First look for the best attack point, then for the collectors to that point and finally decide whether or not the route is feasible. Is it excessively hilly? Are there too many wet marshes? Does the route suit your abilities (Fig. 32).

Fig. 32
Possible route choices

In our example there are three possible route choices, each with its own merits. The safest is C which utilises the path system to the full, as does A, but here the attack point is less reliable as pace-counting is necessary along the final footpath. B is the shortest but relies on the stream junction for a final attack point, which itself is one of two junctions in a marshy area. There is also less climbing involved and what there is, is gradual. Experience, related to the race situation, will decide for you. If things have been going well then perhaps they will continue to, but on the other hand later in the race, if you are getting tired, the problem could be more formidable.

Most route-choice problems in Britain involve utilising the paths, streams and other line features in the first instance and then having to cope with more precise navigation. Each of the three route choices has the possibility of being broken down into several stages but only one has a good attack point. Balancing all known factors, C is probably the best, but then . . .

CONTROL PROCEDURE

Control procedure is the term applied to the phase between sighting the control and leaving it. Efficiency of effort, speed and not disclosing the control position to other competitors you may encounter are the prime factors.

'Efficiency' means a smooth flowing series of actions whilst 'speed' means carrying out the procedures as quickly as possible. Ten seconds lost at every control could mean two or three minutes overall, whilst a minute at each soon produces a loss of 10–15 minutes. Finally the two actions combined effectively will cause minimum disturbance. A smile on the face of a competitor often means he is leaving a control, and so does excessive speed, when previously he was standing around scratching his head!

A good procedure is:

1 Slow down as you approach the control.

2 Know in what direction you must leave.

3 Have your control card ready for stamping.

4 Verify control codes.

5 Punch your control card.

6 Leave in the intended direction.

With practice you should not be stationary for more than a very few seconds.

IMPROVING YOUR NAVIGATION

There are two distinct ways of improving your navigating ability: through continuous competition experience and by specific training exercises. Furthermore, the latter method may be subdivided into theoretical and practical work. If you wish to do well, all three methods should be used regularly.

Practical exercises can be undertaken as part of your physical-training programme. For instance, when going for a long, slow distance run, take a map of a previous race, study it while on the move and make route choices; practice thumbing the map and using the compass. *Fartlek* sessions can be combined with map-memory training, traffic lights and contouring.

Most of the practical exercises involve more than one person – *somebody* must place the controls and others are needed for the actual exercise. Ideally orienteering clubs should organise training evenings with the course-planning alternating between the members. However, if full benefit is to be derived, it is vital that the planner takes the time to study the map and choose good control sites and this task is not necessarily one which can be carried out by all the members of the club.

CROSS-COUNTRY EVENTS

Normal cross-country orienteering events are excellent for training. Potential international orienteers could well use events up to national-badge standard for training whilst those looking only for general improvement could well use club-standard events as training aids. Nobody should treat every event as a race for that way you will never improve your navigation. It will take a lot of self-discipline to continue training during an event, when one of your close rivals streaks past, but remember if you do well in the major competitions nobody is going to question how you do in other events.

Use these events for training by deliberately choosing the difficult routes and attack points and when you make a mistake, stop and retrace your steps until you are satisfied you have remedied your error. Try a few events without the compass or just glance at the map only once between control points. Of course, the less dependent you become on the map and compass the greater chance you have to run faster.

Above all train to race and not race to train.

SHADOWING

In this exercise you require the help of a companion. Whilst you go around in a cross-country event, your companion follows closely behind making mental notes of your route choice, running technique, map-reading and how long you stop for control procedure. If your companion is of a slightly higher standard he will have time to make written notes during brief pauses, or a portable tape recorder can be used. On completion of the run the notes can be studied, related to the map and solutions found to problems which caused loss of time or effort.

FIXED ROUTES

Here a group of two or three evenly matched orienteers is needed. At the start several different but feasible routes to the first control are decided on and one allocated to each person. Starting simultaneously the orienteers move at race pace to the control, the first to arrive noting the time gaps between arriving runners. In this way the advantages of one route over another can be discussed and various criteria for that type of terrain drawn up. For instance, how much detour is permissible to avoid a certain amount of climbing?

It is not necessary to have control markers placed for this exercise, providing the group can agree on each control location and know when they have arrived.

CONTROL PICKING

This involves a course being planned with a large number of controls (Fig. 33) close together: they need not be more than 200–300m apart. The object is to improve control technique and to complete the course with only three- or four-second stops at each control for punching the control card. This type of exercise is often very intense and calls for a good deal of concentration and smoothness of effort.

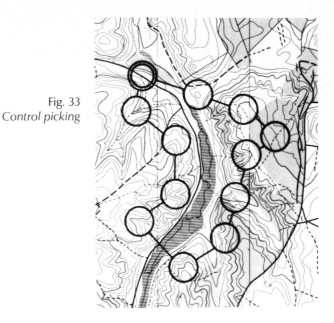

Fig. 33
Control picking

CONTOURING

This exercise can be carried out individually and, as the name implies, involves running at a constant height between two features located at the same height. Initially this should be carried out on relatively regular slope but with experience and practice you can contour around a series of valleys and spurs. Contour navigation is an integral part of any orienteering course and often causes mistakes.

Exercises in climbing and descending a certain height can also be carried out in a similar manner.

One obvious requirement for this exercise is a good orienteering map (Fig. 34) with the contours and features correctly shown.

Fig. 34
Contouring

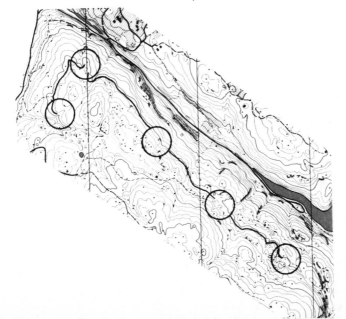

TRAFFIC LIGHTS

A good orienteer must know when to run fast and when to move cautiously. We have already seen that each leg of a course can usually be divided into sections of rough and fine orienteering. In a similar way each section can be allocated a speed of movement.

Green (letter G in map diagram): usually a section of rough orienteering when it is possible to run fast since little navigation is necessary.

Amber (A): again usually rough orienteering but involving more concentration and map-reading and hence a slower speed. An example would be to move on a rough compass bearing but cross several parallel features – a series of paths or streams – and at a particular one locate a definite attack point.

Red (R): always the last part of the leg into the control site but often during other sections of the leg when slow and accurate progress is essential if your exact position relative to the terrain must be known.

Novice orienteers can be given a route of streamers through the forest, the colours changing to red, amber and green as navigation conditions determine. Of course, this exercise should be carried out in conjunction with the map (Fig. 35), so that the runner can see why a particular colour is used. An extension of this is to omit the streamers and mark each person's map with the route shown in the appropriate colours, thus leaving him to navigate and adjust speed according to position on the map.

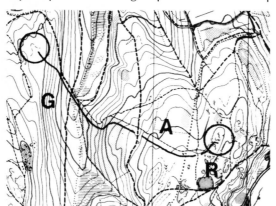

Fig. 35   *Traffic lights*

There are many other exercises which can be practised and many variations of those outlined exist, but if you train regularly your performance should improve.

INDOOR EXERCISES

Indoor exercises should only be done when it is not possible to carry out practical training. They should be treated as an additional learning method rather than as a replacement. Obviously, any time spent studying maps is beneficial but, without the presence of the terrain itself, an essential part of navigation, the decision based on experience, is missing. However, the following exercises can be useful.

All orienteers should keep the maps from their past races for much can be learned from studying your route, relating it to the winner and analysing your mistakes. Over a number of events a pattern of mistakes may emerge and you can then devote some of your training to their solution. It can be useful to keep a diary of events containing the map, results and an analysis of your mistakes.

Map memory
Construct a typical cross-country course (Fig. 36) with the controls a reasonable distance apart, say 400m–1,500m. Study each leg in turn for a period of 20–40 seconds, depending on its length. Then with the map placed face down describe on a separate sheet of paper the route you would take. Turn the map over and check your answer. The studying might involve measuring distance and taking bearings and these should also be included in the period of study.

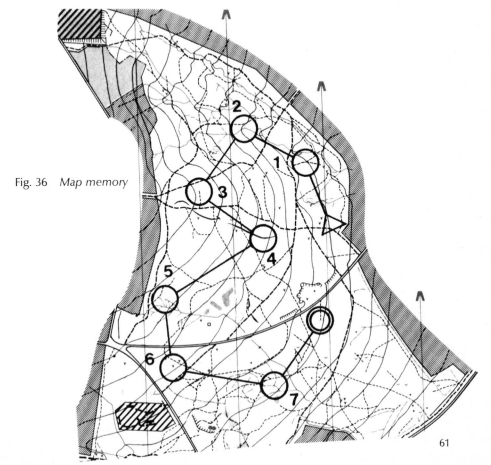

Fig. 36   *Map memory*

Compass use

Using a typical cross-country course take a succession of bearings for all the legs. Obviously this exercise is more easily carried out on a flat table but try if possible to imitate the stance you would use in the forest. You could also use this exercise during a training run. Accuracy of course is essential – an inaccurate bearing is worse than no bearing at all. Distance measurement can also be carried out in the same manner.

Over a period of time you will find it possible to estimate distance simply by looking at the map. You can check the answer using the compass. This skill is of course useful during a race since it allows you to maintain your speed.

The following exercises can be used with a group of orienteers and are particularly useful in a school situation when perhaps the weather is not suitable for outside work.

Route description

One member of the group describes a route on an orienteering map. As he does so, the others try to copy his route onto their maps. There is no need to use control points, for the main requirement is that the actual start is given.

Here is an example:

Follow the stream north for 200m, turn west onto a path and after 50m contour to the boulder . . .

Map bits

Small pieces of map, approximately 1cm square are cut from a map and glued to a piece of card with the direction of north indicated. Each person in the group is given a card and allowed 10–30 seconds for study. The cards are then taken away and each person must accurately plot the position of his piece onto his map. Of course the maps are face down during the period of studying!

Route memory

The above exercise can be repeated using a marked route between control points. The route must then be accurately drawn on to the map from memory.

PREPARING FOR A RACE

This section covers the period immediately prior to a race. It is assumed that the competitor is both physically and mentally prepared for the challenge he is likely to meet.

The preparation can be divided into four distinct parts:
1 Days prior to the competition.
2 The day of the competition.
3 At the competition centre.
4 On the way to the start.

Once a pattern of preparation has been established it is essential that a similar procedure is adopted for all races. All too often races are lost through poor preparation and you cannot expect to perform to the limits of your ability if you are not fully prepared.

Prior to the competition

Make your arrangements for travel. How will you get to the event? What time should you leave in order to allow sufficient time for warm-up, the walk to the start, registration, changing? Allow extra time for traffic delays and other possible problems.

Ensure your clothing and equipment is in good condition. In particular your shoe laces should not be worn – or perhaps still tied in the knot you failed to tackle last time! To have a lace come undone during the race not only wastes time but also disturbs the concentration that is vital if you are to succeed. Is your compass clean and operating efficiently? It cannot be expected to last for ever for the magnetic properties will decrease with use and age. Top orienteers keep one compass for important competitions and relegate the old to training situations.

The pre-race information should be studied, particularly with regard to the length of course, the amount of climbing and the general description of the terrain. This early planning allows you to plan your tactics. Should you conserve energy for the latter part of the race? Will path-running pre-dominate? Is terrain technique important? It can often help to know the different techniques of the planner and mapper for that race – perhaps he favours short legs with little route choice. The types of problems offered might affect your final preparations.

The day of the competition

Ensure you wake up sufficiently early to carry out your final routine. Indeed, if the race is particularly important and you have an early start time, it can be advisable to rise at the same time for a few days prior to the competition. You cannot expect your body and mind to perform at their peak if they are suddenly called upon to function at different times from which they are accustomed. This is particularly so for instance in world-championship competition, when the first-leg runner in the relay starts at 8 am.

Breakfast should be as near your normal as possible but avoid fried foods – the fat can cause stomach problems during racing. The meal should be eaten a minimum of two hours and preferably more before the competition. A good flow of blood through the body and particularly the legs is essential. If some is diverted to aid digestion, you cannot expect peak performance. Change into your running kit and track suit – although you may have allowed sufficient time to do this on arrival, mishaps do occur en route. Any haste, particularly close to the 'off', does not help. Check that the weather is as you had hoped and you are prepared for changes. Finally, leave according to your plan.

At the competition centre

Complete your registration as early as possible in order that you can prepare your map and control card. You can carry the control card in various ways and should already have made your decision during training. The two most favoured by orienteers are within the map case or pinned to the front of the orienteering suit. Both have advantages and disadvantages. A further, less-used method, is to fix it to the sleeve of the orienteering suit and, although there is the possibility of losing it in thick undergrowth if it is not securely fastened, this is a very convenient position.

The map can be prepared by emphasising the top (north) edge with a thick red line. Since orienteering maps usually carry little lettering it is easy to confuse the top with the bottom and hence run off 180° in the wrong direction. The addition of prominent arrows to the north/south lines can also be useful. Many orienteers cover their maps with sticky transparent plastic and although this makes the map totally waterproof there are no distinct advantages over putting it in a good polythene bag. Providing you decide through training and experiment which method is best suited to you – and use it at all times – no system offers any particularly strong advantage.

Finally, study the map. If you were the planner, what course would you set? In particular, look at the 'over or around' problems. Decide how much climbing is preferable to extra distance on paths for this particular area. Are there any areas shown on the map where navigation might be difficult? If so, you are bound to be taken through them, so look at the complexities. Check the printer's register and ensure your copy of the map carries all the intended colours. It has been known for competitors to be issued with maps without the streams being shown, for instance. If the competition centre is on the map then study the area to see how well the map has been made and in particular look at the legend for local variations in the use of symbols.

On the way to the start

Carry out your warm-up procedure – and remember that two or three minutes is not enough. At least 15 minutes of continuous effort is needed. If, during the early part of the race, you find yourself having to think about that slight stiffness in the knee, or your legs and hips are not sufficiently loosened up to clear a gate or fence, or you are out of breath after reaching the master maps, then you cannot expect to make the correct navigational decisions.

A range of exercises and jogging, striding and sprinting should be done before the start but allow sufficient time for recovery immediately before the 'off'. Mentally prepare yourself for the problems. Think about your mistakes in the previous race and think through your tactics.

Above all arrive at the start line ready and keen to succeed.

THE RACE

It is unwise to run hard from the start to the master maps: you will only arrive out of breath and in no fit condition to copy the control points down accurately. Even experienced competitors occasionally make copying mistakes and an extra half minute at the master maps can pay good dividends later in the race.

During your first glance at the course look quickly at the structure of the terrain and make a mental note of the legs where the best route is not obvious. These will require more thought and you can pay particular attention to them during the easier sections of the course. For instance, a long ride between Controls 2 and 3 will provide you with the opportunity to solve the problems of 8 to 9.

When planning the first leg, try to make the navigation as easy as possible in order to allow time to 'play' yourself into the map. Concentrate on the prominent features (collecting features) and choose a good attack point. Above all select a route suited to your abilities. As you progress mentally tick off the collecting features and never put one foot in front of the other before you know where you are.

As you gain experience of the map and course-planning for the competition, you may need to alter your future plans, and the more adaptable they are, the easier you will be able to cope with them – whatever your physical and psychological state.

When approaching controls, slow down and prepare your card for stamping, know your exit route for the next control and try to make your passage from the initial sighting to the correct line of departure as fluid as possible.

During the later parts of the course the experience you have gained earlier in the race will allow you to speed up and improve your route-planning but remember tiredness may set in, lessening your concentration and perhaps resulting in more frequent mistakes. You should, therefore, adjust your speed to suit your condition.

From the last control to the finish along the taped route is the only time you can relax your concentration but remember until you have sighted the last marker, verified the code number, and punched your control card, mistakes can still be made. Do not make the common error of relaxing too soon.

Post mortem
When you have washed, had something to eat and drink you can discuss the various route choices with fellow competitors. It often happens that you missed a vital route choice and lost a few minutes – perhaps something else was on your mind or you could not believe that such a detour was justifiable. Much can be learned from discussion of the winner's route. Pure physical fitness is seldom the reason for success. It is much more likely that the winner's route choice and navigation were superior.

CHAPTER 7

Competition

ORGANISATION

Orienteering is a relatively complex activity and therefore requires more organisation than many sports. It would be beyond the scope of this book to give a detailed account of the duties of all the officials at a major competition but we should briefly outline the main areas of work so that the beginner can have a better insight into what is required to stage an event.

The beginner should have had no difficulty identifying the function of the officials he came into direct contact with at his first event: those who manned registration and the start or took his time and perhaps worked out the results. But, there are important officials the competitor may not meet directly. These are the organiser or coordinator, mapper, course-planner and finally, the controller. At a big competition it may be necessary for several people to share each of these responsibilities but the function remains essentially the same.

The organiser is responsible for the overall administration of the event, and will be involved from the first letter – seeking permission from the land-owner – to sticking the last stamp on the envelopes for the results and the letters of thanks. In practice he delegates much of his work to other people. His is a coordinating role, both before the competition and on the day. He is normally responsible for ensuring that all the necessary equipment is available and that all other officials are briefed and prepared. The organiser usually has little to do, directly, with the construction of the courses and the production of the map.

Most events on the B.O.F. fixture list are run using maps drawn especially for the competition. Chapter 8 will describe what is involved in producing an orienteering map. It is sufficient here to recognise the map-maker's contribution to the organisation of an event. It is extremely time-consuming to survey and draw an orienteering map and is therefore one of the first organisational tasks to be undertaken. For a major championship, mapping might begin three years before the date of the competition. However, with minor events, it is not uncommon for the map-maker to use his detailed knowledge of the terrain and double as course-planner.

The course-planner is responsible for constructing the course, accurately siting the control markers on the ground and producing the master maps. Chapter 9 will describe the main aspects of course construction, but in essence the planner strives to provide a fair test of orienteering skills, appropriate to each class of competition.

One of the difficulties experienced by mappers and planners is that they become so familiar with the terrain that they sometimes find it difficult to visualise the problems that navigators are likely to experience with the map and courses under the stress of competition. This is one of the reasons that events on the B.O.F. fixture list include a further official – a controller. The controller is ultimately responsible for checking that all aspects of the event are organised properly. He is there to protect the competitor's interest – in effect a referee. His major concern will be the course; He/she will ensure that the planner has set a fair and appropriate course for each class; that the course 'legs' test a full range of orienteering skills; that flags are hung in the right place and properly marked on the master map; and that aspects such as safety rules have been observed.

TYPES OF COMPETITION

Cross-country event

In a cross-country competitors visit controls in a prescribed sequence and their performances are directly comparable. Competitions range in distance from 2km for juniors to 16km for élite senior men and it is not unusual for an event on the B.O.F. fixture list to offer as many as twelve different courses. Competitors select the course which best suits their age, fitness and navigational abilities.

In major competitions the control locations would be premarked on to the map but in most other events a master-map system is used. That is, from the start line the competitor normally follows a marked route to a set of master maps, from which he copies the control locations for his course on to his own map. The competitors usually start at one-minute intervals (several minutes in major national and international championships) and must locate the controls in the sequence in which they appear on their map – to take the controls out of order should mean disqualification.

This type of competition gives the course-planner the opportunity to make the best possible use of the terrain, by identifying the most interesting orienteering features and employing them to construct courses to test the widest range of skills. Since, in a cross-country event, the planner is able to prescribe the sequence in which the controls are visited, he knows that the problems he sets will be faced by all competitors on the same course. The principle is that each competitor, by navigating to the same controls, will be faced with, and have to solve, the same navigational problems. This makes for fair competition.

Cross-country events are the most common form of orienteering competition in Britain, although there are often modifications to the master-map system described above.

Multi master maps

When a narrow or small piece of land (Fig. 37) is used for a competition it may be difficult to construct a cross-country course, for which competitors are given all the control locations and descriptions at the first set of master maps. Controls on the outward half of the course will be close to controls for the return portion and competitors may be tempted to visit them out of order. This situation can be prevented by the use of more than one set of master maps. At the first set of master maps the competitor is given only a portion of his course; the remainder will be copied at the second or third sets of master maps. In this way the competitor finding a control by chance is not able to punch his card, as he does not know whether it is on his course. He knows his complete course only after he has visited the last set of master maps.

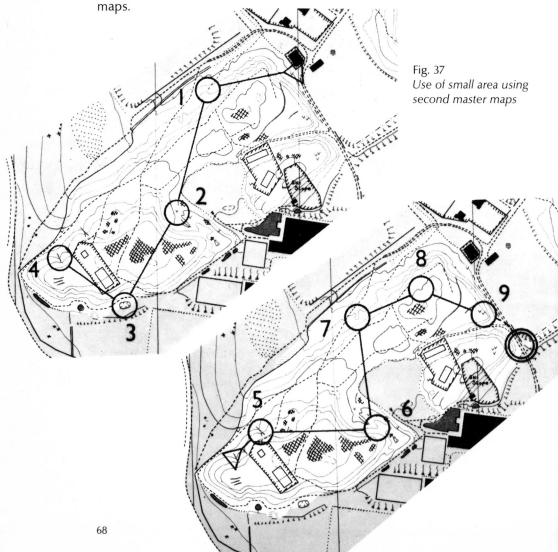

Fig. 37
Use of small area using second master maps

The course-planner is often forced to use multi master maps in order to provide course length or make the best use of a small area, but for the competitor they are an additional tax on energy and concentration. Accuracy in copying from a master map is a vital skill in the sport and becomes much more difficult to perform half way through a course in the stress of competition, with pulse racing and sweat in the eyes.

Norwegian event

A more radical modification of the conventional use of master maps is what is known as the Norwegian master-map system (so called because it originated in Norway). At such an event there are no master maps in the traditional sense. Instead at each control a small section of the map is displayed showing the location of the present control and the next one.

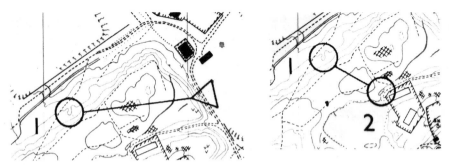

Fig. 38
Norwegian event

The competitor marks his map at every control but knows the location only of the next marker (occasionally two). This type of event is not frequent in important competitions but is very useful for providing a competition on a small piece of land that would otherwise be unsuitable. During the event the competitor may pass many control flags but, since he knows only the location and description of the one he is looking for immediately, other flags are of no value. The total course may criss-cross the same terrain several times, with controls very close together. This would be quite impossible with a conventional master-map system.

Score event

A fundamentally different type of orienteering competition is provided by what is called a 'score' event. In this case up to 30 control points are scattered over the competition area and each control is given a points value according to its difficulty and accessibility. Competitors have a limited amount of time (usually 60–90 minutes) to visit as many of these controls as they can. They are then credited the points value for each control they visit and lose points if they exceed the time allowed. The competition is decided by the competitor's final points score and not the time taken.

Essentially a score event requires the same navigational skills as a cross-country competition but the use of points and not simply time taken makes the competition fundamentally different. The competitor is faced with an array of control sites – probably more than he could hope to collect in the time allowed – and does not have the prescribed route of the cross-country event but must decide the sequence and the controls which he will visit. A variety of permutations and routes are possible and events are often won or lost on the strength of decisions taken at the start about the sequence of controls to visit. Course-planners attempt to provide courses offering a variety of possible routes and, as far as they are able, equal orienteering problems. Inevitably, however, some controls offer easier navigational problems if they are approached from one direction rather than another and there is a certain amount of luck in this type of competition. This is the reason that score events are not popular for championship competitions – there is the luck element and competitors do not necessarily face the same problems.

The pattern Fig. 39 shows the usual arrangement for a score event. Controls close to the start and finish area and those located on large or obvious features given a low points value; those demanding more physical effort or navigational skills to reach are marked higher. Although the excess-time penalty varies according to the relative value of the controls, it is often 6 points for every minute that the competitor takes in excess of the time allowed.

Fig. 39
Score competition

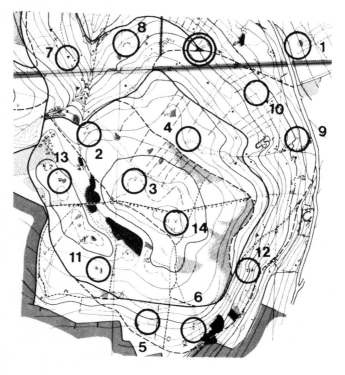

SCORE EVENT		
No.	Description	Points
1	Ditch Bend	15
2	Depression	20
3	Depression	30
4	Ditch Bend	20
5	Vegetation Boundary	45
6	Depression	50
7	Platform	30
8	Foot of Embankment	15
9	Depression	20
10	Ride End	10
11	Clearing (West)	35
12	Outcrop	35
13	Knoll	30
14	Depression	25

Penalty: Deduct 6 pts for each minute late.
Time limit: 60 mins.

A number of features contribute to the popularity of score events. Since the score and not the time taken is the important factor the organisation may be simpler in some senses. The same 30 controls may be used for all competitors: senior and experienced competitors may be given 90 minutes in the hope that the most able may collect them all; junior and less experienced participants may have only 60 minutes. No one could collect all controls in this time so the competition is concerned with the best use made of the time available. Alternatively, the more difficult controls may be excluded from the shorter course, thus keeping the less experienced competitors away from the most difficult terrain. In this way a score event with 30 controls can provide two courses capable of catering for up to 500 competitors, from seven years of age to 70. Organisers do not have to worry about competitors following each other in a score event, since there is no fixed sequence for visiting the controls. Therefore forest cover is not as important and relatively open terrain, perhaps parkland, which may not be suitable for the more conventional type of event, can be used.

The score event has a major advantage when restricted time is available. In a cross-country event competitors may still be in the forest two or three hours after the final start time, but as penalty points are deducted for excess time a score event encourages competitors to return as close to their allowed time as possible. An organiser can predict that within 60 or 90 minutes of the last start time most will have returned from the forest.

With a well-selected central starting position it is even possible to use a mass or group start for a score event. Such an event can be particularly useful at schools, with time at a premium, for it reduces the time spent waiting for one-minute start intervals. A mass start usually requires premarked maps, which should be rolled so that they cannot be read by the competitor – a rubber band or piece of sticky tape on each map is adequate for this purpose. At the start time the maps may be opened and the race begins. Provided a good central position has been used, offering some cover and a variety of first controls an interesting competition can be held with only minimal opportunity for following in the early stages. There is something very exciting about starting in a line with 40 other competitors waiting for the starting whistle or pistol, when all the bodies will disappear into the forest at all points of the compass. If it has been possible to arrange a mass start it may also be possible to have a signal to mark the end of the time allowed – blasts on a whistle or shots from a starting pistol. This can add to the excitement as competitors return from the forest from all directions.

Relay events

If any form of orienteering can appeal to the spectator then it is likely to be a relay competition. Usually relay events involve teams of three runners each running a relatively short cross-country course for each leg of the event. The most common system utilises a central change-over point with the legs of the relay radiating from it. Change-overs are simply a matter of touch between the incoming and outgoing runners. The change-over box is usually staked out with ropes and it is important, when planning the siting of the box, to ensure good visibility so that the incoming runner can be seen as early as possible by his team mate and officials.

Fig. 40
Mass start of a relay competition

A relay competition depends for its spectacle and interest upon the principle that the 'first team to finish is the winner' and it is here that the nature of orienteering causes difficulty. In a normal competition start times are staggered to prevent following and hence the first competitor to cross the line is not necessarily the winner – he may well have been an early starter.

Usually a relay event will involve some form of mass start, similar to that already described. To prevent the first leg becoming little more than a procession following the best navigator, planners and organisers employ a number of devices to break up the field. They may use a variety of first control sites, or a very distant first control with several route choices, or even mix the three legs so that the first runners are not necessarily all running the same course.

There are a number of ways to organise relays. One method, which is useful for a relatively small field, cuts down the amount of following and yet retains some spectator interest, and involves a short break in the proceedings. First-leg runners are started, as they would be in a normal cross-country event, at one-minute intervals. Their times are calculated when they finish and the second runner is started according to the relative performance of his team mate. This requires a short break between the first and second legs but the final change-over is carried out in the normal way. This example illustrates the point.

Imagine the times taken by the first leg runners to be as follows:

Team X	40mins
Team Y	41mins 20secs
Team A	42mins 10secs
Team B	42mins 30secs

The relay would stop at the end of the first leg and a start list for the second runners is then drawn up:

00.00	Team X
01.20	Team Y
02.10	Team A
02.30	Team B

Team X was fastest on the first leg, and therefore has the scratch time. Team Y follows 1 minute 20 seconds later – and so on.

Fig. 41   Change-over at the end of the first leg

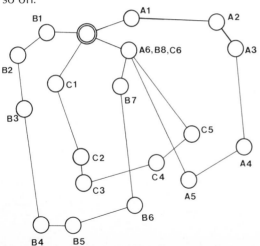

Fig. 42   Typical relay pattern: three legs, A, B, and C

Team events

Relay competitions have the attraction of introducing a team element into what is essentially an individual sport and there is perhaps nothing quite as effective as a source of motivation than the knowledge that other members of the team depend upon your performance. Although they are not commonly used for general competitive events, there are a number of team competitions which might be useful to the teacher or leader – if he should want to tap this source of motivation or interest.

A score event may be organised for small groups – say three competitors – rather than individuals. Thirty controls can be divided among the members of the team as they wish, and the winning team is the one with the highest score. Each control is allowed to score once only for each team and penalty points are calculated in the usual way.

Motivation and interest can also be promoted by the use of a time rather than score team event. As with the score event, a number of controls are located in the forest, but instead of having to collect the highest score in a limited amount of time, each team has to have one of its members at least visit each of the control sites, dividing the total between them. The winning team completes this in the shortest time. The efficiency of the distribution of effort is important. When the teacher or leader knows the teams well it is also possible to handicap them. The authors have used this type of event as a very successful conclusion to a one week's teachers' course and produced a neck-and-neck finish by handicapping the teams on the basis of each individual's competitive performance during the week. Experience also suggests that this type of event is often more popular with young competitors than the normal team relays, which inevitably involve some waiting for other runners to return.

Night events

An orienteer makes his route-choice decisions on the basis of information that he obtains from his map and by observing the terrain he crosses. If you reduce his visibility, you reduce the information available to him and his decision-making is more difficult. This is exactly what happens at a night orienteering competition – the visual check of the physical features of the terrain, which allows the competitor to align his map at speed in daylight, is no longer available. He depends, at night, on his ability to determine the correct direction of travel and accurate distance judgement.

Night events provide a fascinating and sophisticated perspective on orienteering and although it would be unwise to expect complete novices to compete, most people with some orienteering experience find them an enjoyable challenge. One great advantage is that it is possible to use open terrain not suitable for general competitions. Parkland, which can be often found close to city centres, has provided a venue for many successful such competitions. Cross-country, score and relay events can be organised at

Fig. 43   *Master maps at the start of a night event*

night and during the foot-and-mouth disease outbreak in 1969, when all orienteering in open country was stopped, one enterprising group of enthusiasts even organised an urban street event at night.

Safety is a critical consideration in relation to a night event. Because of the additional navigational problems, courses need to be technically and physically easier than those for daylight competition. Course-planners with limited experience should actually plan their courses over the terrain at night, so that they know what they are asking the competitors to do. All dangerous terrain – crags, rivers and unfenced ponds – must be clearly marked on the map and the courses constructed to avoid them as far as possible. Competitors should not be allowed on the course unless they are adequately clothed for the conditions, have a whistle and torch (preferably a headlamp type, with spare batteries) and have already had some navigational experience.

TRAINING EVENTS

The events described in this chapter have been those most commonly used for competitive purposes in this country. It is also possible to use competitive exercises for training purposes.

Line event

In standard orienteering competitions the navigator is given the location of the control sites he is to find and is free to find his own route between controls. However, for a line event, the competitor is given the route or 'line' he must follow. This is marked on his map and he must attempt to keep to this line as he navigates through the terrain. As he follows it he will find a number of control flags – he does not know how many, nor their location, when he starts. As he finds each flag he must plot its exact position on his map. The navigator must be meticulous in the way he follows the route, for if he leaves the line he may fail to see a flag. Even when he finds a flag it is not enough to know that it is situated on a particular feature or bearing. He has to be able to mark it accurately on his map on the basis of his distance judgement. This entails accurate pace-counting. The winner of such an exercise would be the navigator who completes the course in the fastest time with the highest number of controls plotted accurately on his map. There is usually a time penalty for controls missed or wrongly marked.

Corridor event

A line event is a useful exercise to encourage competitors to follow a direct line and develop such skills as travelling on a bearing. In competition it is often an advantage to follow as close as possible to the direct line between controls and a useful way to develop this skill is provided by a corridor event (Fig. 44). A normal cross-country type of course can be set out but, instead of the navigator having the whole map, he is given only thin strips of map between each control. The rest of the detail is blanked out before the map is photocopied. Competitors, therefore, have only a narrow corridor through which to navigate between the controls.

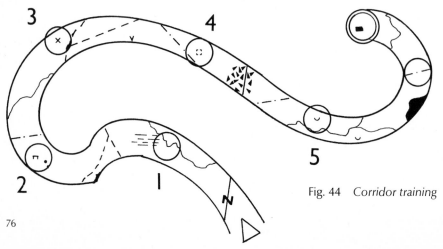

Fig. 44   Corridor training

Window event

The principle of blanking out sections of the map can be used in other ways to develop other skills. Many competitors waste a considerable amount of time making unnecessary stops between controls, instead of making quickly for an obvious collecting feature or attack point close to the control. These intermediate stops can be reduced in training by removing most of the map detail between the control locations and leaving only small 'windows' of map visible (Fig. 45). Since the competitor has detail only of terrain close to the control, there is little point in his making intermediate stops. He must move directly on to the collecting feature or attack point.

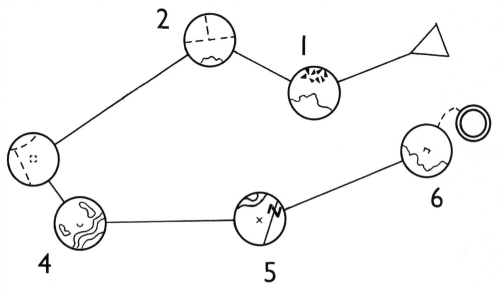

Fig. 45   *Window training*

For experienced competitors the window could show as little as 50m around the control site but a larger area is advisable for beginners – perhaps using a fairly obvious collecting feature – and of course any dangerous terrain on the route must be marked on the map. Controls for this type of exercise must be selected with care: there is no training value for beginners in hopeless failure.

Maps for corridor or window events can be easily prepared and produced, as long as access is available to photocopying facilities. A master map is drawn in the usual way. This can then be placed on a blank sheet of white paper with a sheet of carbon paper between. The required 'corridor' or 'windows' can then be outlined on the map and magnetic meridian lines should also be drawn in at this time. The carbon paper can now be removed and the outline of the windows or corridors is marked on the bottom sheet, together with the meridian lines. The windows and corridors can then be cut out of the paper and the sheet fitted over the map for photocopying.

This type of exercise can be modified and used in many ways. Figure 46 shows the principle being applied to a street event.

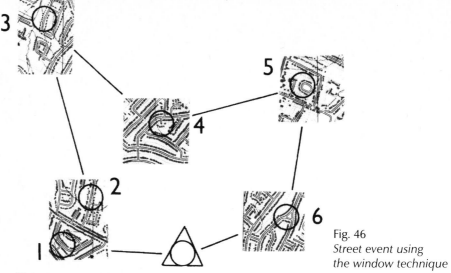

Fig. 46
*Street event using
the window technique*

Streamer event

The principle of a streamer event is that the participant follows a marked trail of streamers, tape or pieces of crêpe paper attached to trees. He is required to relate the terrain he crosses to his map and mark on the map the route he is following. Controls may also be included along the trail and when he finds a marker the navigator must plot its position accurately on his map. The principle has a number of different applications. First, it can be a very useful device for introducing groups of beginners to the forest and is especially useful for young people, for the marked trail provides a safe opportunity for them to get experience of solo navigation. A streamer event may also be of use as a training exercise for orienteers with slightly more experience. A navigator needs to develop good powers of observation, to enable him to recall the terrain he has crossed, so that he may relocate himself if he gets lost. A streamer course can be used to develop this skill. Competitors follow the trail, which should have as many complex twists and turns as possible, at competition speed and without a map. When the competitor returns he must attempt to mark the route he has followed on his map.

Map-memory event

A window event may help reduce the number of intermediate stops that a competitor makes between controls to consult his map, but an exercise more directly concerned with reducing such stops is an event in which the competitor actually carries no map with him. A map-memory event is organised in exactly the same way as the Norwegian event already described. At each control the competitor finds a small map section, showing his present position and the location of the next control. He may carry a compass to orient himself and must memorise the route for the next control – and locate it on the strength of his memory. Should he become lost he must return to the previous control and start again. If map-memory courses are carefully planned they can do a great deal to wean beginners from un-necessary and time-consuming consultations of the map. It may be advisable to allow younger competitors to carry a map in their pockets – only to be consulted in an emergency – to increase confidence.

PERMANENT COURSES

This chapter has described a variety of activities and competitions that are possible in orienteering. One of the problems with the sport is that before it is possible to have a meaningful orienteering excercise it is necessary for someone to go into the forest and mark the control sites. This is usually done almost immediately before the competition is to take place and can of course be time-consuming. It means it is not always easy to stage a small training exercise because of the amount of work involved.

During the last few years Britain has seen the growth of a number of permanent courses. Unfortunately they are still scattered but their numbers are growing, thanks to the cooperation of such bodies as the Forestry Commission and efforts made by a number of orienteering clubs. The idea is that in an area of forest, for which an orienteering map is available, a number of control sites shall be semi-permanently marked – with painted stakes or some other durable marker. Usually each marker carries a code and the course can be used by any individual or group for training purposes, if they make arrangements to buy the map. An ideal example is the Forestry Com-mission Camp Site at Beddgelert in North Wales. A full five-colour orienteer-ing map of the surrounding forest is available, with 26 control sites marked with wooden stakes and pin punches. Maps and an information sheet can be purchased from the camp shop (for 30p). The course offers an excellent introduction to the sport for beginners, training for the experienced com-petitor and a ready-made competition for the teacher or leader with the group staying at the camp site.

Many Scandinavian countries have developed the recreational aspects of orienteering into a national Trim Orienteering scheme. Most large towns have a semi-permanent orienteering course within easy reach, and it is possible to buy a Trim pack from shops or garages close to the course. The pack contains a map of the course and details of the scheme, together with information for people trying the activity for the first time. The purpose is to develop the wayfinder recreative aspect of the sport, as well as provide some exercise for serious competitors. There is nothing really competitive about the scheme, but when a person has collected the codes from each marker on the course it is possible to send away for a simple Trim Orienteering badge and this provides a little interest and motivation, especially for the young.

CHAPTER 8

Mapping and orienteering

PRINCIPLES

Orienteering is navigation around a set course of given control points. It follows therefore that the basic tool, the map, should represent the terrain as accurately as possible. A requirement of any competitive sport is that as far as possible the same conditions should apply to all. If circumstances vary for different competitors then the competition cannot be described as fair. In a given orienteering situation the competitor can only make decisions based on the information provided by the map. Should that information prove to be incorrect an unfair advantage may be gained by some competitors. Our example (Fig. 47) may illustrate this point.

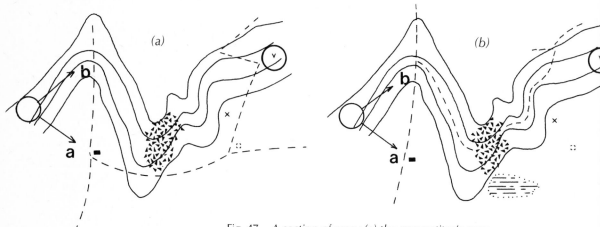

Fig. 47 *A section of map: (a) the competitor's map,*
(b) the actual terrain

On the left-hand side is the map used by the competitors in the race, whilst on the right, we have the situation actually encountered.

Orienteer A has made what appears to be a good route choice, but because the footpath no longer exists the time he takes to reach the control point is greatly increased. Orienteer B appears to have made a bad route choice, certainly – on the basis of the information provided by the map – a much slower one as it necessitates contouring around a steep hillside. However, since the original survey was carried out a new path for forestry operations has been made and he is now fortunate enough to have a good surface to speed him on his way. B has thus gained an unfair advantage. Some will argue that this is part of orienteering, that luck should play a part in the result, but surely this has little to do with competitive sport.

In orienteering the competitor who has mastered all the skills and success-fully applied them during a competition should be the winner. It follows then that the greater the opportunity the course-planner has to test these skills the greater the likelihood that the best competitor will triumph. With more detail accurately shown on the map the planner has more opportunity to present orienteering challenges. A map used for an orienteering competition should be accurate enough to enable the competitor to use all his navi-gational skills, principally those of map-reading, direction-finding and distance judgement. We shall see in the next chapter how the quality of the map will affect the role of the course-planner. When choosing control sites and assessing route choices the accuracy of the map is of paramount importance to the planner.

In Britain, when orienteering started in the early 1960s competitions were usually held on Ordnance Survey $2\frac{1}{2}$in to 1 mile maps or on the larger 6in to 1 mile. Although these maps are excellent – indeed the best of their kind in the world – they have many shortfalls as far as orienteering is concerned. The forested areas generally used for competitions are often not mapped with sufficient detail for a competition to be fair. The small detail necessary for good navigation is not shown and the information which is present is often out of date. As orienteering in this country became more established and more competitors were travelling and competing overseas on good-quality orienteering maps, so the demand for better maps grew. By the late 1960s the demand was so great that O-maps began to be produced by orienteers and by 1970 it was unusual to compete using a map which had not been improved in some part.

In the last five years the quality of mapping has increased considerably and the sport is now beginning to attract not only competitors but those with an interest in mapping. However, such is the relationship between mapping and competition that we are unlikely to develop the competitor–official relationship found in many other sports. To be a good mapper you also need to compete, for it is only then that you begin to understand the problems that can occur.

FEATURES OF A GOOD MAP

The ideal orienteering map is one which shows:

1   All line features (i.e. roads, tracks, paths, boundaries, streams, ditches).

2   Vegetation (i.e. forest density, undergrowth, open land).

3   Point features (boulders, pits, depressions, ponds, marshes).

4   Shape of the ground (contours).

If you are embarking on the production of your first orienteering map the above should also represent a priority for surveying. It is most important that a resurveyed map used for a competition is consistent in the detail it gives the navigator. The competitor should find that the ditch he crosses shortly after the start is shown on his map, in the same way as a similar feature anywhere else on the course. It sometimes happens that a mapper runs out of time or enthusiasm and decides that there are too many similar-sized features – ditches, knolls, depressions or boulders perhaps – for them all to be surveyed. Consequently the map may show only those he had surveyed at the beginning of his work. But it is important that the competitor finds consistency in the features depicted. If the mapper decides that only knolls over 5m high are to be shown on the map, then a knoll of 3m should not appear and no knoll over 5m should be omitted.

Line features are the first and most important additions and corrections to be made to an orienteering map for, as we saw in an earlier chapter, route choice depends greatly upon these and their use as handrails or collectors. They are also the easiest amendments to make to the map, for having established their beginning it is relatively easy to plot length and direction.

Secondly the vegetation – not necessarily its type, although in some circumstances this can be useful information – particularly its density and the speed at which it can be crossed is crucial information. As we saw in the earlier diagrams a planted area in its early years can seriously affect your route choice. Not only the thickness of vegetation affects speed. The going underfoot – nettle, bramble and bracken – all play their part in influencing the result of a competition. Changes of vegetation can also be usefully plotted for they provide additional navigational aids and control locations.

Thirdly, the point features need to be shown. These may be good control sites for the more difficult courses but require accurate plotting, often the result of many hours of meticulous ground survey.

Finally, and for many people the most difficult part of mapping, comes the interpretation of the shape of the ground into contours that the orienteer can quickly understand. On most topographical maps contours are accurately plotted using modern surveying equipment. The interval is regular and precise and small changes are often ignored as they may fall between contour lines. For instance, if the contours of a hillside are 25ft apart but between them there exists a small re-entrant of a depth of 20ft this would not appear on the map, even though it might make an ideal control feature.

It is particularly important for the contours on an orienteering map to look right to the competitor. If the ground steepens in a particular place, though technically it would fall between two contour lines, it is preferable that the contour lines on the orienteering map be 'adjusted' to take account of this. Similarly with the small re-entrant mentioned earlier. The example (Fig. 48) may illustrate this point.

Figure 48a shows the hillside represented by accurately surveyed contours whereas 48b includes the 'adjusted' contours to take into account the small re-entrant which falls between the 'correct' contours. Orienteering maps also make use of 'form lines' to represent height loss or gain that might not be shown by standard contour lines

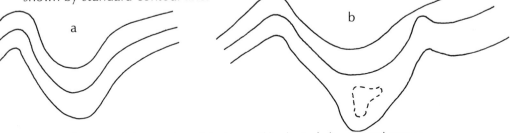

Fig. 48   *Contours: (a) as on the original map, (b) adjusted after ground survey*

Requirements of an orienteering map

It should be:

1   Up to date.

2   Consistent.

3   Accurate, within the limits of the provisos mentioned.

4   Clear and legible.

5   Include as much detail as possible, but bear in mind 2, 3, 4.

6   Free of information that is not of benefit such as unnecessary names and heights of hills.

We have already looked at the reasons for accuracy and consistency but it is vital that whatever the quality of the finished map it be clear and legible. In this respect the quality of drawing is very important. Often a good survey has been spoilt by 'sloppy' drawing. The right equipment should be used for, as with all items produced by craftsmen, the appearance of the finished product is directly related to the type of tool used in the manufacture. You cannot expect to produce a good map using a paint brush or felt-tip pen.

The map is also easier to read if it omits information not of direct benefit to the competitor. The names of houses, woods, ponds etc., are obvious examples. Seldom is such information available to the competitor on the ground, so why include it on the map? Similarly, the practice of including contour heights is unnecessary. An orienteer is concerned only with the rise and fall of hills and valleys relative to his position on the map and can do this quickly by counting the number of contour lines. As the competitor becomes more experienced this too becomes unnecessary for he begins to have a feel for a map and can project a picture of the terrain in his mind.

Scale

In the previous section we saw that one of the requirements of an orienteering map was that it should be clear and legible and it is in this respect that scale is a matter of concern for both mapper and competitor. A map possessing all the other qualities is useless if it is not printed at the correct scale. Nearly all orienteering maps are printed at 1:20,000, 1:15,000 or 1:10,000, the choice depending upon the quality of drawing and the amount of detail shown.

As has already been mentioned, before embarking on the drawing of a map it is necessary to decide what scale is to be used. If, for instance, the map is printed at 1:10,000 it would require not only a large piece of paper but would also increase both the labour in drawing it and the cost of printing, whereas printing at 1:20,000 might mean that small detail is confused or obscured.

If a competition is to be held on Ordnance Survey maps then there is little choice available, the main scales in use being 1:25,000 ($2\frac{1}{2}$in to 1 mile) and 1:10,560 (6in to 1 mile) – or 1:10,000, depending on the date of the survey. The large scale has a number of advantages, particularly of clarity, but has the disadvantage of showing contours at 100ft intervals, and that only on land below 1,000ft.

Certainly the popular 1in to 1 mile, or the more recent 1:50,000 should never be considered for serious competition. Very little useful information is available to the orienteer from maps on these scales. Competitions held on them will be unfair in nature and thus produce an invalid result.

What type of map?

Several different types of map are possible for an orienteering competition, ranging from a photocopy of the Ordnance Survey map to a first-class coloured orienteering map. They differ in cost and quality and are suitable for different standards of competition. A map suitable for a world championship requires a far greater degree of accuracy and thoroughness than that for a small local competition although the participants in the local competition would not object to a map of championship quality! However, it is wrong to assume that the lower the standard of competition the lower the standard of the map may be. An introductory event for beginners must have an accurate map. The major difference would be in the type of land used.

Let us consider the different types of maps available.

1   Ordnance Survey map.

2   Photocopy of the O.S. map.

3   Photocopy of O.S. map with minor amendments.

4   Orienteering maps.

The first three relate to existing Ordnance Survey maps. There is little to choose between 1 and 2, the only differences being colour and cost. To supply each competitor with the original O.S. map would necessitate an entry fee of over £1, whilst by using photocopies this cost can be reduced dramatically. Before photocopying, however, it is necessary to ink in some of the features, particularly the blue colouring representing streams, ponds and lakes. This should be done by using a good-quality drawing pen of diameter 0·2mm, and simply drawing over the top of the existing blue line. Many photocopying machines cannot reproduce the colour blue, this being most noticeable in the case of streams and ponds. An infinite number of copies can be reproduced though once more than fifty copies are required the off-set litho process should be preferred. Besides each copy being cheaper, the finished product has greater clarity.

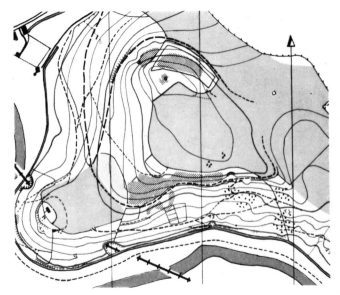

Fig. 49
Ordnance Survey at 1:25,000 and an orienteering map at 1:10,000 of the same area

Prior to photocopying you might improve the look of the finished product by including additional information on the sheet – the name of the club or school promoting the event, the scale, contour interval, some safety instructions, magnetic variation and so on. Remember all copies from O.S. maps must have the permission of the Ordnance Survey and credit should be acknowledged on the maps.

Even if you are fortunate enough to have an up-to-date O.S. survey of the area you are to use it is likely that some amendments will have to be carried out prior to reproduction of the map. It is possible that the area you have chosen has no Ordnance Survey map available though this would only be the case for the more remote, little populated areas. In these cases the only solution for the novice mapper is to choose a different area which has the required information.

PRODUCING A MAP

There is no greater satisfaction for the mapper than to see his finished product in print. On the first occasion, this experience can be likened to locating your first red-and-white marker. It is something you never forget but unlike the marker, which soon becomes just a memory, the map will always be there to remind you of your toil, both in the forest and at the drawing-board. Both aspects, the surveying and the drawing, are extremely satisfying in themselves but seeing the finished product is something every orienteer should experience.

It is important that for a first attempt a suitable piece of land should be chosen. Ideally it should be a small piece of woodland or common within easy reach of your home. A square kilometre is quite sufficient for a local orienteering competition, indeed courses of 5–6km can be set in such areas, provided they have sufficient control locations. Try to find an area which is not too contoured, contains a reasonable number of line features, a limited number of point features and reasonable consistency of vegetation, density and undergrowth.

Having located the area you wish to map, the first task is to trace the owners and explain what you wish to do and why. It is upsetting to spend hours mapping an area only to find the landowner is not willing to allow you to stage a competition on it. Most landowners are happy to allow you the use of an area, particularly if during your negotiations you impress on him that you are concerned about his land and the countryside in general. If it is an area where shooting takes place then it always helps if your request for a date for the competition takes note of the breeding and shooting seasons. February, March and April are particularly good times for the orienteer, since both the undergrowth and the problems caused to game are at their lowest.

Your second task is to choose the scale and here it is often useful to compare your area with others of a similar nature already having orienteering maps. The number of colours on the finished map should also be considered. In general, the greater the number of colours the clearer the map, but remember the increase in colours will also increase the cost of production, since in conventional map-printing each colour is applied separately. It is probably best to consider a simple black-and-white map in the first instance, but before you make the final decision look carefully at the improvement you might gain from the addition of a second colour, whether it be brown, green or yellow. It is worth noting that a black-and-white map does not omit the blue (water) detail but simply uses a different symbol or line thickness. However, too many thicknesses of lines or different symbols can be confusing and result in a poor map. It may be necessary to omit certain detail – the difference between a ride and a track, or degrees of vegetation density, for instance.

BASE MAPS

With these decisions made, your first task is to prepare a base map on which your surveying can be carried out. Ideally this map should be at twice the final scale of your finished map. For example, a final scale of 1:20,000 requires a base map of at least 1:10,000. Similarly, one of 1:10,000 requires 1:5,000 – and so on. Generally speaking, your base map will be the appropriate Ordnance Survey with the appropriate enlargements. These maps are ideal in that they provide the fixed reference points on which all your surveying will be based. They may not have the smaller detail you require for an orienteering map but the positions of the boundaries, trig. points and roads will generally be correct.

Enlargement

Several methods of enlargement of the base map are possible. Some are more accurate, some more expensive, but in decreasing order of merit these are:

1   Having an off-set printer make a plate at the designed enlarged scale and then print several copies.

2   Have a photographer make an enlarged print and then reproduce several on a copying machine. With this method it is important that subsequent enlargement does not take place, as can often happen when a copying machine is used.

3   Produce an overhead projector transparency and then project to give other designed enlargements on to your base-map material and then draw over the projected outline.

4   As 3, but this time using an episcope.

5   Usually the most inaccurate enlargements result from using a geometric grid system.

The base map now produced could be used for surveying in the field but, before embarking on this phase, it is worth trying to improve the quantity and quality of detail with information from other sources. Make use of other maps and air photographs, and land managed by the Forestry Commission or by a private estate may well have maps of the area showing forest roads, types of trees, dates of planting, drainage systems, together with plans for future new roads, planting, felling and so on. This latter information can save many surveying hours later on. If such maps are available it is worth remembering that they may not be as accurately surveyed as you would wish. They should therefore be treated only as a guide to what is there.

AIR PHOTOGRAPHS

The two main uses of air photographs, as far as the orienteer is concerned, are to provide supplementary information for the base map or new map construction on a photogrammetic plotting machine. This latter use is too specialised for the scope of this book and is covered in other publications.

Because an air photograph (Fig. 50) does not differentiate varying heights the scale across a photograph will vary, the basic principle being the nearer to the camera the larger the scale and thus, as with estate maps and the like, air photographs should be used only as a guide. They will show what exists but its exact position will vary according to its height; similarly land to the extremities of the photograph will also vary in scale.

Fig. 50
Aerial
photograph

The time of the year and indeed the time of the day can affect the usefulness of the photograph to the orienteer. Ideally the photographs should be as recent as possible and have been taken during the spring when there is little undergrowth or leaf cover. This will then allow you to see more ground detail.

The main uses of air photographs are thus:

1   Location of point features.

2   Verification of other base-map information.

3   Guide to vegetation type and density.

However, remember that all the information should be taken as a guide only and will need to be accurately plotted by ground survey.

The sources of air photographs are many but two registers now exist which contain comprehensive information on all air photographs.

To make an enquiry, send a tracing of the area from the 1in O.S. map and on this indicate the outline of the particular area, giving the O.S. sheet number and grid lines.

The information you will require is:

1   Details of all flights of the area.

2   Scale of the photography.

3   Date of flight.

You will then receive a list of flights, together with details of the source of the photography. For England and Wales you should write to:

>Central Register of Air Photography
>Prince Consort House
>Albert Embankment
>London SE1 7TF

and for Scotland:

>Air Photograph Library
>Scottish Development Department
>York Buildings
>Queen Street
>Edinburgh EH2 1HY

SURVEY EQUIPMENT

The base map, or preferably a copy of it, together with all the other information you have managed to collect from other sources, should now be fixed to a hardboard base-board and drafting film or paper fastened over it. Drafting film is preferable, as it is stable in all weather conditions and less opaque. Several types are available but those with a matt surface on both sides are better.

The base map and board, together with a pencil and an orienteering compass, are the only essential items to produce a perfectly good map.

However, life can be made easier by the use of a good sighting compass, where an accuracy of half a degree can be obtained whereas the former is only likely to give an accuracy of $2°$ – but then this is usually sufficient for a first map.

Other equipment such as clinometer, tape, wheel, altimeter, theodolite etc. can be used but in general the accuracy which they give is not necessary for an orienteering map of reasonable quality. The major requirement of a map is that the position and size of features, relative to all the other features, is correct.

THE SURVEY
Distance measurement
When carrying out a survey you are principally concerned with measuring the ground in terms of distance and direction. Direction is determined by the use of a compass, whereas distance can be determined in a number of ways:

1   Pace-counting – either a metre pace can be practised and used or your

natural walking paces which can then be converted to metres. Knowing you take, for example, 56 double paces for every 100m you can devise a scale to attach to your base-board and then carry out the necessary calculations as you progress.

2   Chain – this is much too awkward for use in wooded terrain and its accuracy is much greater than is really needed.

3   Tape – easier than a chain and sufficiently accurate for the orienteer's needs. It is however more time-consuming than pacing and does require two people to operate it.

4   Wheel – much quicker than a tape and over smooth terrain as accurate. Its use should be confined to roads, tracks and paths with fairly good surfaces. It is quite easy to construct a 1m wheel and a counter can be incorporated as well.

5   Optical range-finder – rather expensive and often not suitable for use in woods, as short distances and poor light conditions are often the norm.

Usually then, pace-counting is sufficient but, as with pace-counting in a competitive situation, a lot of practice is required in order to achieve a good level of accuracy, particularly in steep terrain.

Recording the information

Two types of information will need to be recorded during the survey: detail plotted on to the base map and notes made during the survey. The information drawn on to the base map is best done using a number of coloured pencils – blue for water and marshes, black for tracks and paths, brown for contours, knolls and depressions, green for vegetation, and so on. This simplifies the later task of transposing your information to the base map. All types of notes can be made during the survey – bearings from a point to a particular object, directions of streams at crossing points, vegetation density, comments about sections of terrain you can see but will not survey until later. These notes are best made in a rain-proofed notebook available from drawing-office suppliers. This avoids the problem of the page disintegrating in the wet.

Initial survey

During the initial survey of the whole area you should decide such matters as which features are to be plotted, what constitutes a large path, what a small path and what a ride. This is particularly important when several surveyors may be used. It is no use plotting, for example, all the 1m boulders in one area and omitting them in another, because there are a number of 2m boulders.

Remember that one of the basic requirements of a good orienteering map is that it should be consistent over the whole area. Do not fall into the trap of including a number of small features in one section because there is little else there.

Finally, if there is the possibility of insufficient time being available, establish, before you begin, an order of priority for the detail:

1 Roads, tracks, paths (features which help progress).
2 Cliffs, thickets, marshes (features which hinder progress).
3 Other line features (fences, streams, ditches etc.)
4 Point features (boulders, depressions, ruins etc.)
5 Contours.

Fixed points

Following this initial survey it is necessary to establish a number of fixed points whose position has been checked for accuracy and which can be used for fixing further detail. In average British terrain this is best done by plotting the track and path network. This will give you a number of fixed points, such as path junctions. The plotting of this network will also subdivide the area into a number of smaller compartments, enabling the surveyor to work on one part at a time.

In order to plot a path the following method should be used:

1 From a known fixed point take a bearing along the path to a point where it bends or, in the case of a long straight feature, as far as you can easily see.
2 Sight on to an obvious marker at this point.
3 Note the bearing.
4 Pace along the path to this point and note the distance.
5 Repeat the operation from this new point.

This exercise is then continued until a new fixed point is reached. In this manner the whole path network can be plotted (Fig. 51).

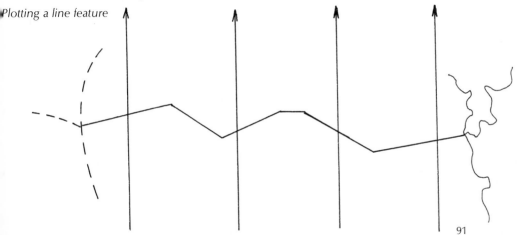

Plotting a line feature

When pacing along a path you can also make notes about other features you pass – for instance a stream which passes underneath, a path junction, point features visible in the forest. It is useful to take a bearing on these features at this time so that you do not miss them when you come to survey the detail within the network.

Having established the path network, the other line features can be added – the streams, fences, ditches etc. – again making notes on point features observed. Vegetation boundaries are plotted in the same way as line features but you should also note the density in order that the finished map can indicate the speed at which it can be crossed. Ideally this applies not only to trees but to rhododendron, bramble, nettle and bracken.

Point features are plotted by sighting on to two or more known points. This is a quick and accurate method and solves the problem of pacing, particularly when the ground is rough or steep. In order to locate point features simply walk up and down the area in a regular fashion. It is not good enough to give a casual glance around as you may miss a feature which a competitor subsequently sees and thus loses his confidence in the map. Sight on to two identifiable points, or preferably three; the intersection of the lines on the base map giving the location of the feature.

Occasionally it is not possible to see a fixed point from the feature and in these circumstances the competitive technique of aiming off (Fig. 52) can be used.

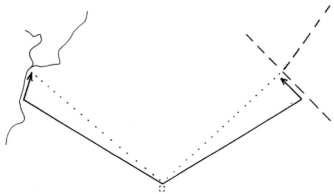

Fig. 52   *Determining the position of a point feature*

From this point feature take a bearing from the map on to a line feature. Follow this bearing until the line feature is reached, then pace along the feature until a fixed point is arrived at; by reversing this operation on to the base map it will be possible to plot the line along which the feature lies. Repeat in another direction on to another line feature. The intersection of the bearings then gives the point.

In time, the experienced mapper can carry out a lot of his survey by eye and consequently complete his work in a much shorter time but with the same degree of accuracy.

Contours

To most people, the improvement of the existing Ordnance Survey contours is the most daunting of prospects. However, if you adopt the attitude that the apparent shape is much more use to the competitor than the exact situation, the task is much simplified. Providing the height difference is accurate and the contours are close together when the terrain is steep and far apart when it is a gentle slope, the main requirements from a competition standpoint are catered for.

Features on hillsides – spurs, re-entrants, gulleys – can be plotted in the same way as point and line features. The end of a contour feature can be determined as a point feature and its direction as a line feature. Similarly for its width. The contours can then be adjusted as previously described.

The information collected during the survey can be added to the base map during the evening, using both the notes made and features plotted on the covering sheet. In this manner the base map can be completed over a period of days or weeks. On its completion, the final drawing preparatory to printing can be carried out.

DRAWING THE MAP

All drawing must be done on drafting film as the material used must remain stable in varying conditions of heat and moisture. Drafting film can be obtained from all good drawing-office supply shops as can the drawing pens required. The type most commonly used are Rotring Variant and nib sizes of 0·2, 0·3 and 0·4 are suitable for most of the work.

Your base map should be fixed to a smooth flat surface and a sheet of drafting film fastened over it. Each colour in your final map will require a separate piece of a film, although the information will always be traced in black ink and for this Rotring or Pelikan TT inks are ideal.

While drawing, the film should be kept completely free of grease, particularly that from your hands. As you trace information, errors will undoubtedly occur but these can be removed with a sharp razor blade. Lines such as those representing footpaths should be drawn as continuous and then, when dry, scratched away to produce the dashed effect. Since the tracings are being prepared at twice the final scale, inaccuracies resulting from the hand shaking will disappear, but remember that features too will be reduced by half.

During the drawing stage the magnetic-north lines should also be put on and a normal compass can be used to give the required angle. Letraset, or similar self-adhesive lettering, should be used for the wording as this enhances the look of the finished article. Letratone can be used for the vegetation density, out-of-bounds areas, open areas etc. Simply put an approximate sized piece on to the area to be covered and cut around the perimeter with a razor blade – being careful, of course, not to damage the surface of the film. The remaining pieces can then be scraped clear.

If you are preparing a multi-colour map register crosses must be placed in each corner of each piece of film. When the crosses are aligned, streams should flow down valleys and under bridges, the open areas fit into the fence system – and so on.

As the drawing progresses you should think about the final result. Leave room for the title, scale, O.S. copyright notice, date of survey and, of course, the legend. You might finish the map off with a border and perhaps use the club or school emblem.

Printing

On completion of the drawing check that nothing has been omitted. that there are no unsightly errors and the completed map looks presentable. Your map is now ready for printing.

Each sheet of film should be marked with the colour it is to be printed and the top indicated.

The printer must know the exact size it is to be and this can be done by telling him the final distance between the magnetic-north lines or the register crosses.

Ensure he knows the exact tones of colour you want and here a past orienteering map would be useful as a sample.

He also needs to know how many copies you want – and remember the more you order the more the unit cost lessens. Agree a delivery date and finally, when you have received and are satisfied with the finished product, pay the bill!

CHAPTER 9

Planning the courses

Many factors contribute to a successful orienteering event: the terrain, the map, the start, finish and results service but no amount of efficiency in these particular fields can compensate for a badly designed course or incorrectly located controls. Providing that the start and finish arrangements can cope with the timing to the nearest second for each competitor, it is then the partnership of the course and the map which most influence the result. Some may argue that the map is the most important aspect of an event because it is from the map that the competitor derives his information and makes his decisions but even if the map is poor a competent course-planner can utilise those parts of the map which are correct for his planning and still produce the best orienteer at the end of the competition.

OBJECTIVES

He must strive for a balance between the elements of speed and navigation. However, the ideal balance is seldom possible and therefore sections of the course where navigation is simple and speed plays a dominant role should be compensated for by sections where navigation is difficult and movement at speed impossible.

The main objectives of the course-planner are to produce:

1   A fair course.
2   A challenging course.
3   An interesting and varied course.

A FAIR COURSE

Several factors affect the fairness of a course but of prime importance are the map, the terrain, the types of legs and the control sites. We have already looked in detail at the map, which should first and foremost indicate how easily a piece of ground can be crossed. It should be detailed enough to allow accurate map-reading, particularly around the control points, and, finally, be of even quality and reliable.

Different types of terrain test different skills. Ideally, a course should test the full range of orienteering skills but in Britain the available forest and terrain mean that this is seldom fully possible. A flat featureless forest will suit one competitor, whilst a rugged mountainside will be preferred by another. It is for the planner to draw upon his experience as a competitor and official to make full use of the terrain he has at hand.

The types of leg can vary from a simple single route choice involving the following of a track to that of a multi-choice situation requiring good map-reading. The more route choices, the greater the possibility of spreading the competitors and reducing the opportunity of following and thus offering a fairer course.

Finally, the accuracy of the control sites and the fixing of the flags are important considerations. The height and the way that the flag is hung, together with the size of the feature relative to the nearest attack point, all affect the fairness of the course.

A CHALLENGING COURSE

A course can be challenging in many ways but of prime consideration are the physical and mental challenges provided by the terrain and the navigation. Steep terrain provides a major challenge to old and young competitors alike but to a fit athlete it is of secondary importance compared to the state of the ground cover. Boulders, bracken, brambles and nettles all affect his performance and it should be remembered that the difficulties caused by the vegetation vary according to the physical stature of the competitor. A ten-year-old of 5 or 6 stone will find 3ft high bracken or brambles a much greater hindrance than a 6ft, 12 stone man.

The mental challenges also vary according to the age and experience of the competitor. A seemingly simple route-choice situation can provide a major problem to a youngster on his first competition, and we shall see later how to plan specifically for the varying abilities and experience of competitors. It is vital that all competitors should be able to enjoy and complete their course. Little satisfaction can be gained by the planner or competitor when the results list shows a large number of retirements.

AN INTERESTING COURSE

Interest and variance in a course are also the trade marks of a good planner. The shape (Fig. 53) of the overall course is of importance here. It is much easier to cope with a course which has a shape similar to that of Fig. 53b than it is to cope with one which has a shape similar to that of Fig. 53a. It is easy to settle down into a routine of bearing slightly right out of a control and navigating for three or four hundred metres as in the former whereas the latter calls for fresh thinking at the beginning of each leg as to direction and length.

Interest too can be lost when the control features are always similar, for instance, when only spurs and re-entrants are used. Try if possible to intro-

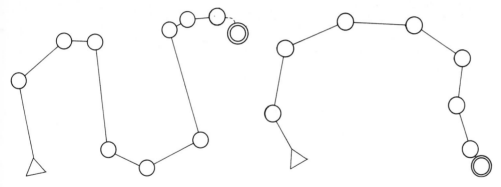

Fig. 53   *Course shape: (a) good, (b) poor*

duce variety in features – stream, boulder, ruin, marsh etc. – for different features often require a change in your navigational approach. If possible the terrain should be varied – uphill, downhill, contouring, flat, and undulating. All provide different problems and solutions.

CHARACTERISTICS OF A GOOD COURSE

Having looked at the task of the course-planner let us now consider the characteristics of a good course. Remember a good course is one which continuously and adequately tests the physical and technical abilities of the competitor at a level appropriate to age, sex and ability. This is best achieved by varying the following elements:

1   Terrain.
2   Type of leg.
3   Length of leg.
4   Direction of leg.
5   Control features.

Often the planner is not called in to perform his skills until the competition area has been selected and perhaps even the map has been produced. Such circumstances limit the scope available but if he has experience in his craft and gives thought to the problems posed by the terrain he should still be able to produce, fair, interesting and challenging courses.

TYPES OF LEG

The types of legs you can offer between control points can usually be varied. In order of priority you should test:

1   Map-reading.
2   Route choice.
3   Compass and distance.

Accurate map-reading requires skill and experience gained in many competitive situations and is closest to the definition of pure orienteering. Route choice too is derived from skill and experience but once the decision is made little remains but to convey yourself from one control to the next. Of course the ideal is a combination of both. On the other hand, compass and distance requires little skill or experience and also tends to allow following, something always to be avoided in orienteering.

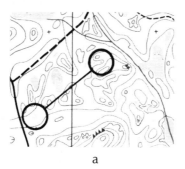

a

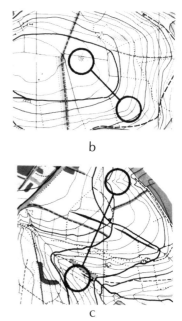

b

c

Fig. 54
Sections requiring different techniques:
(a) map reading, (b) compass and distance,
(c) route choice

The length of legs can and always should be varied. Certain navigational skills can only be tested with certain leg lengths. With a leg length of between 100 and 200m the solution is nearly always compass and distance except when, with suitably detailed terrain, map-reading might also be involved. Route choice in this situation is seldom tested. However, short legs are indispensable as an aid to producing a varied course with direction changes and should therefore not be discounted. A sudden change from a long to a short leg and vice versa has often led to the downfall of a competitor.

The direction of leg can also be varied but in some circumstances, more notably on the shorter courses, not very significantly. It is important to change the direction as much as possible but all the time be aware of the other mistakes that can be made. With constant changes of length and direction there is a greater possibility of the less skilled competitor making errors of compass and distance measurement.

Finally let us consider the types of control features. They should be varied as much as possible to help make the course interesting but the size of the feature, relative to the ability of the competitors and to its distance from the nearest attack point, must be considered carefully. It would be very unfair, for example, to have a control on a 1m square boulder at 300–400m from an attack point if there were no other features between them to navigate by. Even the most skilled user of the compass would be unable to accurately locate the boulder except by luck, and luck produces unfair results.

CONTROLS

In considering the question of fairness and its application to controls the following points should be taken into account:

1   Accuracy of the control sites.
2   Suitability of the control sites.
3   Visibility of the control flag.
4   Availability of attack points.

The principal requirement is that the control be in the correct place. It must be placed exactly on the feature which lies at the centre of the control circle marked on the master map to which the control description refers. It is also essential that the physical feature which is to be used as a control site is indicated on the map – how can a competitor be expected to navigate to unmarked features (or for that matter transfer correctly the circle from the master map to his own map)? With the high-quality orienteering maps in use today there is no longer any need to use indefinite features with consequential lack of accuracy. Using the less reliable Ordnance Survey map there is always the risk of placing a control in the wrong place. However, whatever map is used, the method for determining the control positions is basically the same.

The control must be correctly placed with respect to the map. That is, the feature you wish to use in the terrain is the one shown on the map and the other features shown on the map around the control feature are also correct. Remember a competitor will be using these features to navigate his way to the control point. This also applies to features on the far side of the control from the likely direction of approach. A good planner does not wish to penalise further any competitors who have already lost time by overshooting the control and having to return (Fig. 55).

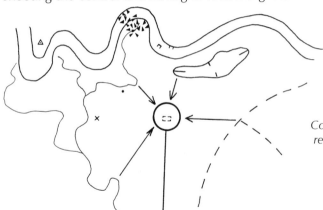

Fig. 55
Control must be correctly located with reference to the possible attack points

The control must be suitable for the skill of the competitors using it. A control suitable for an advanced men's course will not be suitable for a children's novice course. The examples (Fig. 56) on the right of a small crag and boulder in a well-featured area is not suitable for novices, whereas those on the left of a path junction and stream are ideal.

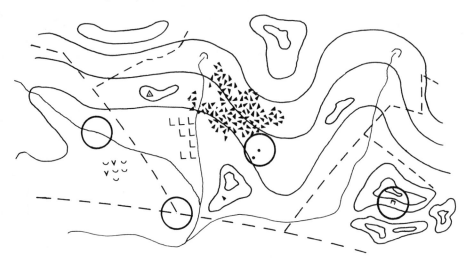

Fig. 56   *Controls for a beginners' course: left-hand pair suitable; right-hand pair unsuitable*

Controls in thick forest or flat featureless terrain as in the diagram are far from suitable, for instead of requiring skill they become more a matter of luck. Such controls are often referred to as 'bingo' controls. The visibility of the control – that is the distance from which the marker can be seen – can have a significant effect on the result of the competition. In general, the feature should be seen before the marker but occasionally the quality of the map, particularly with regard to the features around the control necessitates the marker being more prominent than might otherwise be the case. There is always argument as to how the marker should be hung when a depression is used as a control feature. With this type of control there is always the possibility that an approaching competitor locates the depression by observing a fellow competitor 'popping up' out of the ground. If this situation is likely to occur, it is best to dispense with the control or alternatively hang the marker in such a way that it is visible whether another competitor is there or not.

A marker should be hung fairly so that once the correct feature is located, it can quickly be seen. If a feature such as a boulder is used and a marker is visible only from certain directions of approach, or it is not possible to discern from the map on what side it is placed, the description should indicate at what point the marker is hanging – 'west side', 'north-east corner', and so on.

Remember also that it is never sufficient to check the accuracy of siting of the control points only. Since all controls are approached from attack points, these too must be given attention, and this also applies to all attack points – not just the ones you personally might use. Orienteers are diverse in nature; all must be catered for.

Remember the essence of orienteering is navigation at speed; the controls serve only as a turning point in order that fresh navigational possibilities can be presented to the competitor. It follows, therefore, that every control must have a specific purpose. It is not sufficient merely to place controls for the sake of it.

A course-planner, in placing a control, does so in order to create a good leg or possibly, when the terrain dictates, just move competitors from one place to another in order that another good navigational leg is created. In Fig. 57 the inclusion of Controls 2, 4 and 7 serve this purpose. For if Control 1 did not exist the leg from the start to 2 would cease to have any navigational interest. However, with 1 and 2 in position the leg from the start to 1 is good, as is that from 2 to 3. Although 1 to 2 is not so good, it is short and a small fraction only of the total course. Naturally, if you can plan a course without these short legs, so much the better – but beware you do not fall into the trap of producing legs of similar lengths with a regular change of direction.

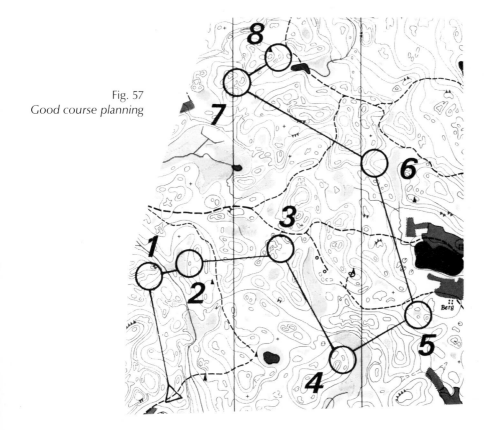

Fig. 57
Good course planning

Any control with a purpose is justified but every control with no function reflects a failure of the planner to understand the philosophy of orienteering. Of course, it can be very tempting to hang controls in difficult and intricate terrain – but only if it serves a purpose. The number of controls you use will vary from one forest to another. There is no set number, no ratio of control points to length. A forest based on a grid pattern might require a large number if any navigation is to be presented. On the other hand, in a well-featured, undulating forest only half the number might suffice.

Above all, when you have constructed the course look at each control and leg in turn and ask yourself 'What would happen if I took that control away?', or 'Can I amalgamate those two into one or those three into two?'

START AND FINISH

It is most important that from the timed start to the timed finish as much as possible of the course presents navigational problems. The placing of the start and finish is, therefore, as important as the placing of the controls. First-class orienteering should be provided from the very beginning and in this respect it may be necessary to place the start some distance from the car park and competition centre. In Scandinavia, for major competitions, this is sometimes as much as 3km. Providing competitors know this well in advance and can allow sufficient time they will not be unduly concerned. A marked route can be used for the competitors to follow in order to get themselves to the good terrain. After all, it is much better to walk gently to the start of a good course than to have to run through bad terrain.

The actual start should be situated so that none of the possible route choices leads competitors who have started back through those waiting. It is better if the start is a fixed feature on the map as this then allows navigation to begin immediately. Master maps, if used, should be placed as near to the start as possible, for it is negative orienteering to have to follow tapes, but at the same time the master maps should be out of sight of waiting competitors. They should not be able to see in what direction others have gone.

The positioning of the finish is critical, in that all competitors must be timed correctly and, therefore, the finish officials must have a clear view of approaching competitors. To assist in this it is usual to have a taped route from the last control but this must be kept as short as possible. In addition, the direction of the taped route should be marked on the master maps, otherwise a competitor might accidentally come across the tapes and then backtrack to the control. To navigate to the tapes is one thing; to come across them accidentally, another.

A scenic finish is always desirable from the spectators' point of view but it should not be at the expense of course quality.

STREAMERS

On occasions it may be necessary to ensure that competitors use a specific route between two points. In this case streamers can be hung for competitors to follow. The position of both the beginning and end of the streamer section must be marked on the master maps, which ensures that the competitor is not left wondering about his position at the end of such a stretch.

It must be stressed, however, that marked routes (Fig. 58) should never be used except in special circumstances since they allow the competitor respite from navigation.

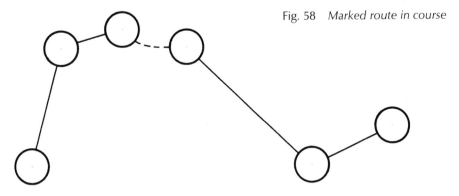

Fig. 58   *Marked route in course*

DOG-LEGS

A dog-leg is simply a situation in which the same route is used both to approach and leave a control. In these instances the exact location of the marker can be given away to an approaching competitor by one who is leaving. An experienced entrant can use this situation to his advantage. Of course, this is possible at all controls but in a well-planned course this would be penalised since the approaching competitor would have to cover extra ground in order to reach the far side of the control feature.

Figure 59 shows a situation in which a competitor missing the control on the left side must then run in ever-decreasing circles in a vain attempt to locate the feature, whereas a competitor missing to the right will eventually be shown the direction by outgoing runners.

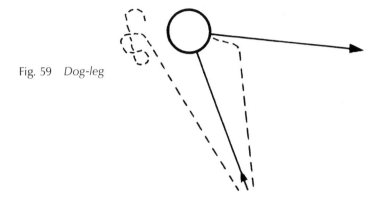

Fig. 59   *Dog-leg*

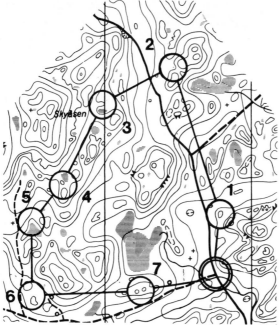

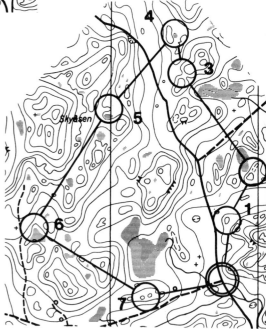

Fig. 60   *Avoiding dog-legs*

The two maps (Fig. 60) show, firstly, on the left, three dog-leg controls whilst that on the right, by having additional controls near at hand, eliminates the problem. Remember, though, that solving the problem in this way may create others for you – you may now be faced with two short non-orienteering legs. Although this is an improvement on the original, further modifications may be possible.

COLLECTING FEATURES OR LOST DISTANCE

It was shown in an earlier chapter that a good way of simplifying the navigation was to look for an easily locateable feature near to the control site. This would then permit orienteering with less thought and probably allow for faster running. Consequently, as a planner, you are likely to avoid this situation (Fig. 61).

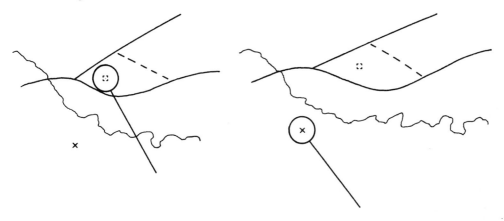

Fig. 61 *Controls sited in relation to collecting features*

In the examples, the first illustrates a poorly placed control and the other a well-placed one. The former permits coarse navigation for the majority of the leg, whilst the latter ensures that the competitor is made to orienteer. There are occasions, however, when it is advisable to have the first situation – for instance when planning for relatively inexperienced competitors and juniors. Often then it is best to situate the control between two large collecting features.

OUT OF BOUNDS

Often there are areas where competitors are not permitted – cultivated fields, newly planted woodland etc. – and the areas involved would be marked on the maps with cross-hatching. To then set a leg with a route choice through such an area is asking for the area to be entered, either accidentally or deliberately. It is not sufficient to assume that all competitors will use the 'obvious' route choice. Such areas should be avoided by a reasonable margin and this is particularly so for juniors, who will often not know their precise location – and it is easy to confuse open, rough land with newly planted areas.

DOUBLE RUNNING

Two or more courses at the same event can cause additional problems.

Often some controls are common to two or more courses and, although a particular situation may not be a dog-leg, on one course it becomes so when an additional course is considered (Fig. 62).

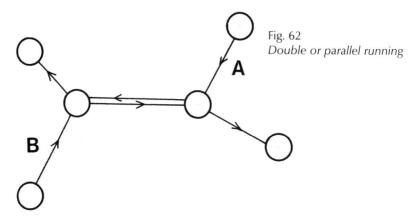

Fig. 62
Double or parallel running

The diagram shows clearly that an orienteer on course *A* could easily be shown the location of the control by an orienteer on course *B*. Similarly Controls 2 and 3 are identical on both courses although on *A* navigation is from 2 to 3 and on *B* from 3 to 2.

PLANNING FOR JUNIORS

There are several reasons why extra care should be taken when planning courses for juniors but most important of all it should be remembered that most juniors are – or have recently been – beginners. It is therefore essential that their new-found interest is retained and developed. If the occasions on which they miss controls or fail to complete the course are more than rare they will soon lose interest.

The acquisition of skills in orienteering takes a long time and, if courses are not properly planned, little enjoyment or success will be achieved, but, having learnt the basic principles, the young orienteer can complete simple courses.

Of course there are many juniors who are excellent map-readers, having learnt at school or in a youth association. You will then often hear complaints about how easy the course was, that the controls were on large and easy features and they ask to move up to a more demanding course. It is at this stage that many juniors are allowed to move up a class too quickly. Analyse the situation and try to discover how much of the time was spent standing or walking whilst making decisions on navigation. Remember orienteering is 'navigation at speed' – most people can navigate given a good map and time. It is important that juniors learn to navigate a speed whilst the problems are relatively easy for to move on without having mastered this basic skill can mean only slow development, if any, in the future.

Recommended winning times for juniors vary from 20 to 45 minutes depending on age and sex, but it must be remembered that the tail-end of the field is likely to be completing the course in one to one and a half hours, and perhaps even longer.

There is considerable pressure to increase the recommended winning times, particularly at the younger age end of the classes. A comment often expressed is that to travel for up to two hours to an event for a 20-minute race is hardly worth the effort but to increase the length means slowing the running speed with a resulting bias towards navigation and not orienteering. A junior's physical capacity is relatively low and underdeveloped, and although running tempo can be high it is seldom maintained as endurance will not have developed. An exceptionally gifted junior can always move up a class, whereas you cannot move a junior down.

Ideally, up to three courses should be available in each class – a novice and two others of appropriate length for the more experienced, with a move up a course being governed by ability and experience. However, the ideal is seldom possible and a middle-of-the-road solution is to provide one novice course for all beginners.

Planning courses for juniors is difficult, harder in many ways than for experienced seniors. All planning is largely dependent on local conditions but, if novices are the major group to be catered for, the terrain you choose should reflect their needs. Ideally, this should include both cultivated and wooded land, but all should be easily runnable and the whole area surrounded by easily identifiable major features – for example, a road network, fence system or water features. At all times the map should be clear, simple and depict large features.

The existence of route choices is not necessary as at this level of performance the task of reading the map is a problem in itself. Controls should be large, easily identifiable and linear in nature. At all cost, point features should be avoided – even large depressions are not suitable. The marker itself should be hung so that it is visible from all directions of approach and, if necessary, undergrowth around the marker should be cleared away. Between and behind the controls there should be good collecting features to prevent the novice from straying too far from the course. It would not be extreme for the first few legs to be connected by a single line feature – for example, a control on a stream bend, followed by a control on the same stream but at a junction 200–300m away.

Short legs are more important than long as there is less likelihood of the competitor straying when faced by only a single route choice. Above all, the novice competitor must enjoy the course and be successful.

For more experienced juniors, the terrain can be totally wooded but must still be 'runnable'. The orienteering difficulty should not be too great and although large features between controls can be omitted it is still advisable to have collecting features at the back of the controls. Longer legs can now be included, and route-choice problems introduced, but the markers should continue to be prominently displayed and visible from all directions of approach.

It is difficult to achieve the right balance at this level and constant discussion with the competitors and other planners is needed if courses of the correct type are to be constructed.

Occasions do occur when unsuitable terrain has to be used. In these instances the problem is usually solved if a large number of controls are used; or the control is placed on the far side of a large collecting feature; or the course keeps close to prominent line features. For detailed information on recommended course lengths and winning times see Appendix C.

Courses for juniors must keep well clear of major hazards – such as crags and deep marshes – and, as far as possible, out-of-bounds areas. It is not sufficient for these to be clearly marked on the map, for the young competitor rarely knows his exact position with an accuracy better than a couple of hundred metres.

Control sites and markers should be hung high enough for young children to see, while they must, of course, be able to reach the punch.

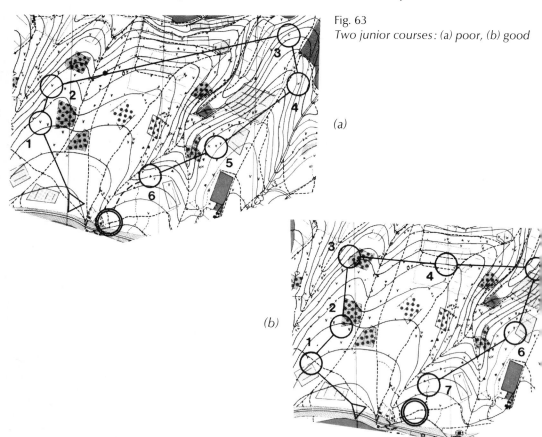

Fig. 63
Two junior courses: (a) poor, (b) good

(a)

(b)

CHAPTER 10

Orienteering
for teachers and leaders

The nature of orienteering meant that it quickly appealed to teachers and youth leaders as both an individual and group activity – hence the car park at most events usually contains a fair number of school and club mini-buses. The emphasis in the previous sections of this book has been upon individual aspects of the sport. We should now consider some of the problems and possibilities associated with introducing other people to the activity. Orienteering tends to turn its participants into passionate disciples who are anxious to spread the word and, whether you are initiating 'the neighbour and his kids' or an organised group, a number of principles should be borne in mind.

BASICS

As a very minimum, before you take any beginners to an orienteering event, as a responsible and experienced competitor, you should satisfy yourself that each individual is adequately prepared. For a start, this means he must be suitably clothed, have a whistle and be fully aware of safety rules and the 'Country Code'. He must also have had sufficient instruction and experience to complete the course he/she intends to enter. Remember beginners tend to overestimate their ability so ensure that they enter an appropriately simple course and check their map after they have been to the master maps. If you have done your job properly, beginners should not need to retire from their course but, if they do, it is your responsibility to make sure that they report to the finish.

Orienteering can be very rewarding as a group activity, for both group members and the leaders, but if the leader does not fulfil his obligations to prepare the beginners, there can be disaster for all concerned. Beginners, especially young people, can get lost, become anxious and disheartened and may want nothing more to do with orienteering. Meanwhile, the leader waits at the finish, wondering how it can take anyone four and a half hours to complete a course of less than two miles. Serious competitors have their concentration broken by beginners asking for advice and eventually the organisers, who are already quite busy enough, may have to arrange a search party. Such fraught situations can be prevented if group leaders – and indeed anyone introducing newcomers to the sport – does so responsibly. Introduce them to the sport informally, before letting them enter competitive events. To arrive at one with a large group of complete beginners is to invite disaster.

The British Orienteering Federation has established a Coaching Award Scheme, the purpose of which, at the instructor level, is to give teachers the basic experience and information required to introduce beginners to the sport (see Appendix F). But above all practical experience is vital. Before bringing in new faces, teachers and leaders should ensure that they have adequate experience themselves. It is no use talking to others about navigational problems until you have solved some yourself under competitive conditions.

STAGES OF DEVELOPMENT IN SCHOOLS

In Scandinavia, orienteering is part of the compulsory curriculum for all children of more than seven or eight and assumes an importance over and beyond that simply of a sport. It is unique in its potential as an introduction to a wide range of educational activities, for it involves the mathematics of bearings and angles and the basic tool of geography and environmental studies – the language of maps. We are slowly beginning to realise the educational potential of orienteering in the United Kingdom but a detailed consideration of this aspect is beyond the scope of this book and we shall have to restrict ourselves to orienteering as a part of sports and outdoor-activity programmes.

In this context in the school we might consider three distinct 'stages' of development or three levels at which the teacher and students might be working:

Stage 1
Preliminary navigational skills. This level is concerned with the children developing an understanding of the basic skills of navigation, skills which are not exclusive to the orienteer but are common to all forms of navigation practised with map and compass.

Stage 2
Simple competitive skills. This level is concerned with children understanding the rudimentary competitive skills concerning route choice and applying these in a competitive situation. This would involve skills such as aiming off, the identification of collecting features, the use of attack points, and the like.

Stage 3
Advanced competitive techniques. This level is concerned with the coaching of competitors who have substantial experience and helping to develop more sophisticated techniques, both mental and physical.

We shall now consider these levels in a little more detail. Stages 1 and 2 are primarily concerned with group teaching, while Stage 3 is more concerned with coaching the more experienced and competent and has much in common with the material discussed in Chapters 5 and 6.

ORIENTEERING IN SCHOOLS LEVELS OF DEVELOPMENT

Orienteering in an educational context can be considered in three general categories, each representing a different level of development:

STAGE 1	STAGE 2	STAGE 3
Preliminary navigational skills	Simple competitive skills	Advanced competitive techniques
Developing the basic skills of navigation common to all map and compas navigation.	Developing simple competitive skills and applying these in competition.	Coaching competitors who have substantial experience and developing more sophisticated techniques.
	1 Ability to identify and use: collecting features, handrail features, attack points and the skill of aiming off.	
1 Understanding the map: symbols, plan, relief and scale		1 Development of individual performance both technical and physical.
2 Understanding the compass as a measure, to set the map and to take bearings.	2 Ability to identify and solve: route-choice and detour problems.	2 Development of the skills of map memory, terrain memory, contouring and control picking.
3 Relating map to ground with and without compass.	3 Development of appropriate: physical fitness with stress on orienteering as a *running* sport.	3 Development of individual schedules and routines for training, preparation and racing.
4 Development of distance judgement: the step scale and thumbing the map.		

STAGE 1: PRELIMINARY NAVIGATIONAL SKILLS

Before anyone can enjoy orienteering as a competitive sport they must have a grasp of the basic skills of navigation, as outlined earlier. Experience suggests that whatever the age or apparent sophistication of the group introduced to navigation, it is very easy to overestimate their grasp of these skills. Even while working with groups of teachers we have found it worth-while to deal thoroughly with simple matters before progressing to the more complex skills.

In Chapter 2 we discussed maps in terms of the use of symbols and the concepts of plan, scale and relief. It is not difficult to introduce beginners to the notion of the map as a simple plan. A progression from a plan of the classroom, to the school field and then to the immediate neighbourhood can be used to develop such an understanding. One of the quickest ways to help the young understand maps is to have them attempt to make one. We have found that a very useful device is to give children an outline, or alternatively a partially completed map, and have them fill in the detail. This will require an understanding of distance, scale and the use of symbols. They can be given a plan of the school corridors and asked to complete the detail by adding certain features, such as fire-alarm bells, windows and cupboards. A partially completed plan of the school field could have paths, outbuildings and perhaps large trees accurately located upon it and – when compass use has been introduced – the position of goal posts and jumping pits could be accurately plotted.

Large-scale plans of the immediate neighbourhood of the school can usually be obtained from the local authority and the 6in and 25in Ordnance Survey maps are ideal for introducing basic navigational skills. A simple competition can quickly be staged on such maps, using postcards as control markers.

The most difficult aspect of map understanding to teach is relief. Navigational errors made by young beginners often stem from a misunderstanding of the contour system. There is a limit to the value of the teaching aids which can be used to develop this facility. It might help to take a local O.S. map and plot a relief profile of an area, so that the children are able to relate the contour systems on the map to the hills and valleys of the terrain that they know well. The use of a relief model might be of value but map understanding is a practical exercise and is probably best taught in the field. To teach a group of children the meaning of contour lines, have them walk the hills and valleys that the contour system represents.

There is some division of opinion about the best time to introduce the compass to beginners. Our experience convinces us that it is a hazard to do so until the novice has a sound understanding of maps. Although the compass is an admirable instrument, it is no more than an *aid* to mapreading. Orienteers use their compass in three main ways and this can provide a useful sequence for introducing the use of the Silva-type protractor compass to beginners.

Firstly the compass can be used as an aid to distance judgement, a measure, and the beginner can produce an individual step scale and fix it to the leading edge of the compass. The compass may then be used as a magnetic instrument to allow the beginner to align north on his map with magnetic north and set or orient his map. Once a beginner can judge distance with the help of a step scale and orient the map by using the compass, he has the basic skills required to complete simple orienteering courses. He can then move on to using the compass to take and use magnetic bearings but this should be left until the pupils have a sound understanding of maps and the simple skills described above. It is all too common to see novices hypnotised by the wonders of the little red needle on their compass. They take a straight-line route on a bearing that even the most elementary understanding of the map should tell them to avoid.

Remember at this stage to keep your teaching simple and not technical.

There are a number of simple games and exercises which can be used and although they may have little direct carry over to the practical orienteering situation, have been found to be useful as devices to familiarise beginners with the compass itself.

Exercises for simple compass work

There are three simple steps in the use of a protractor compass, (see p. 33). In the first two, the navigator uses the compass on the map to obtain a magnetic bearing and the third involves moving on that bearing through the terrain. The steps are essentially very simple but do require some care and experience is the best teacher. The following exercises give practise in these skills.

1 Taking a bearing

Exercise Orienteers seldom, if ever, look at the numerical value of the magnetic bearings they use but it is possible to set an exercise making use of these numbers. Draw the outline of an orienteering course on to a sheet of paper, include a series of parallel lines to represent the magnetic meridian lines on a map and add the other detail. This can be photocopied or produced on a stencil for duplication. Each player is given a copy of this sheet and a compass, and timed while he takes the magnetic bearing for each leg of the course, which he enters into the answer column. The bearings should then be checked and a 'penalty' of ten seconds added for every two degrees of error.

Purpose:
   Practise for the beginner in taking a bearing.
   Teacher can identify those likely to have difficulty taking a bearing in the field.

2 Moving on a bearing

When the beginner has mastered the skill of taking a bearing from the map the teacher will want to give him experience of moving on that bearing.

Exercise a Hunt the Penny. The simplest exercise for moving on a bearing requires the beginner to place a coin, or any small marker, at his feet, so that he knows his exact starting position. He must dial a bearing on his compass, preferably less than 90° and walk for a given distance, say ten double strides on that bearing, and stop. He adds 120° to the first bearing then dials this on his compass. He then walks for the same distance on this new bearing, stops, adds a further 120° and walks for the same distance on this bearing. If the exercise has been performed accurately, the player should have walked around three sides of a triangle and returned to the spot he started from. The exercise can be modified. If, instead of 120°, 90° were added at each corner, a square would be formed. 60° would produce a hexagon – and so on. (The number of sides of the figure divided into 360° will give the bearing to be added at each corner.) As players gain experience so the distances can be increased.

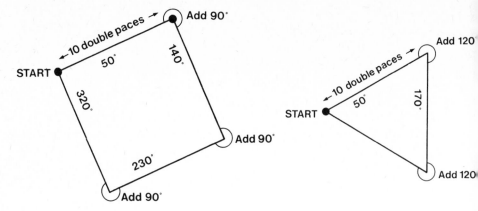

Fig. 64

Hunt the penny: another exercise for improving bearing and distance measurement

Exercise b   School Yard Compass Game. Silva Compasses market a game which can be played by up to 20 people and involves bearing and pacing exercises (see Appendix E for address).

Purpose (a and b)

Beginner develops skills required to move on a bearing, especially handling and holding the compass.

Even when working with large groups the teacher can identify those not holding the compass properly and correct the error at an early stage.

Exercise c   Cross-country bearings. More direct orienteering practice can be provided. The teacher must identify a number of straight collecting features – tracks, fences or even streams – and place a series of numbered markers along these features at regular intervals – say 20–30m. Each player is given the bearing from a known starting position to one particular marker (he does not know the number). He then travels on the bearing to the feature and notes the number of the nearest marker. The winner is the player with the smallest error. A number of these exercises can be linked together to form a short course.

Purpose

Provides experience for beginner travelling on a bearing, moving to the collecting feature. The exercise is safe for young children.

Allows teacher and beginner to identify any individual tendency to move to one particular side when travelling on a bearing.

3   Bearing and distance

It is only half of the navigator's problem solved when he is able to travel in the right direction; he must also know how far he has to go. There are several exercises that combine the skills of using bearings and distance judgement.

Exercise a   A miniature event. This exercise is usually carried out in a fairly open wooded area but with very young beginners it is probably a good idea to have a 'dry run' in a field before moving to the forest. A games field can also be used for the exercise at night with more experienced navigators. Arrange a number of markers in a pattern. Each marker should give a bearing and a distance, indicating the location of the next card. If the markers form a closed circuit, it will be possible for a player to start at any marker and return to that point.

Exercise b The above exercise can be modified to relate more directly to the orienteering context. Instead of giving the competitor the bearing and distance to the next marker, at each card a map section shows the distance and direction and the competitor measures these as he would in a conventional competition.

Purpose
To develop techniques of precise bearings and distance judgement.

At the completion of the preliminary stage teachers might expect the children to have an understanding of the map, the use of symbols, and the meaning of plan, scale and relief. They should also know how to use the Silva compass as an aid to map-reading (i.e. as a measure and as a magnetic instrument by which to set the map and to take and use bearings).

It is difficult to generalise about this level. Older children who have been taught the basic principles of map and compass well, before they come to orienteering may need only quick revision but experience suggests that it is all too easy to overestimate the grasp beginners have of these skills. It is as well, when trying to introduce novices to orienteering, to spend time establishing the fundamentals of navigation, for a sound understanding of basic skills pays off when progressing to more complex techniques. Not every child will want to take part in competitive orienteering but the basic skills of navigation have a general application to education and outdoor pursuits. There is a strong case to be made, on grounds of safety alone, that the basis of all outdoor-activities programmes should be an understanding of the fundamental skills of navigation with map and compass as described above.

STAGE 2: SIMPLE COMPETITIVE SKILLS

When children have an understanding of the basic skills of navigation it is possible to get down more directly to orienteering. But whatever you do it is important to keep the fun and enjoyment. This is easier done if beginners experience success. This should be ensured by progressing from the very simple skills. The 'sink or swim' approach, where children are just sent into the forest inadequately prepared is likely to mean failure for all but the most able. At this stage it is important to develop confidence as well as technique. Beginners need to develop a trust in the map and their ability to use it. The tasks they are asked to perform should be relatively simple and within their ability.

Frequent reinforcement is important and courses for beginners should contain a high number of simple controls so that there is the satisfaction of finding a flag as often as possible. With very young children it is particularly important to ensure that they do not spend long periods lost – a dark forest can be frightening to an imaginative young mind.

If a teacher wants to develop the competitive sport of orienteering, he needs to ensure that the children have a grasp of the basic skills as soon as possible, so that accurate route-choice decisions can be made at speed. Orienteering, remember, is a competitive, *running* sport! Easy courses with many controls and little chance of serious error will encourage children to run. If this is emphasised early, the beginner is less likely to develop the habit – common among many novices – of spending long periods of time immobile consulting the map. There is a fine balance to be struck here. If beginners are encouraged to run before they have mastered the basic skills, they will make mistakes, become lost and perhaps lose interest in the sport. On the other hand, if they are not encouraged to run as soon as possible, they may develop the habit of stopping and standing immobile to consult the map before every route-choice decision. Running and competition should be used carefully to increase the efficiency of decision making on the move.

It is extremely important at this stage to set courses of the appropriate length and difficulty. In the early days of orienteering we (as experienced competitors) often set courses that were totally inappropriate for beginners, especially young people. We are now able to see that short courses with obvious control sites and simple navigational problems are what we should provide. Particular attention should be paid initially to the availability of handrail and collecting features. It is especially useful to site controls on junior courses with substantial collecting features behind the marker, to give an immediate feedback of error. Another factor which is important to bear in mind when setting courses for beginners is concentration span: it is not realistic to expect juniors to concentrate for more than about 20 minutes and if courses are much longer than this they are probably counter-productive and encourage poor technique.

Inhospitable terrain can add to the fear many young people have of a dark forest. High bracken or bramble may provide no real check to the progress of an adult but it might be a very real obstacle to and restrict the vision of a junior. The young, particularly girls, may feel more comfortable when beginning the sport if they take part in pairs. There is no reason why they should not do so, but it is important that the teacher ensures that they both have a map and both do the navigation. When they have developed confidence and competence, they can take part as individuals (see pp. 106–8 for discussion of course planning for juniors).

The second stage in our sequence is concerned with the beginner's introduction to competitive orienteering. We have discussed some general points above and now look at some of the skills which characterize this stage of development and some ways they may be approached.

The development of basic competitive techniques depends on the beginner's ability to understand the map and orient it to the ground. This skill, together with the development of distance judgement, is of initial concern. The most effective way to develop such skills is to give children practise navigating with the map. The production of individual step scales (described on p. 30) can be a useful preliminary to this. Many young people find distance judgement extremely difficult and if they have a means of relating their stride length to distance on the map and on the ground, it is a great help in coming to terms with the problems of practical navigation.

Ideally, each beginner could be asked to navigate around a simple course with an experienced competitor on hand to discuss the physical features of the terrain and explain the skills of orienting the map and checking progress by thumbing the map. However, in a school context, this one-to-one relationship is seldom possible but much can be achieved in a small-group situation and don't forget you can use experienced senior pupils to help the novices.

It is possible to start with a 'map walk', with the teacher simply leading the group through the forest and attempting to reinforce basic navigational skills by discussing general aspects of the terrain, possible control sites, collecting or handrail features and the use that could be made of them. It is important to stress that each individual in the group follows the progress on his map by marking his position with his thumb and that the map is kept in the set position. The teacher can stop periodically and ask the group to hold their maps in front of them and those who are unable to set their maps or track their progress by using their thumb are quickly obvious. This type of activity can be extended in a number of ways:

a *Follow my leader*   The speed of the map walk can be increased until the children jog, and finally run, following the teacher. Throughout, each must attempt to keep his map in the set position and his location marked by his thumb. Members of the group may alternate as leader, giving the teacher a chance to check the progress of others within the group. This exercise can be modified when coaching more advanced techniques.

b *Streamer event*   In this exercise the teacher marks a route with streamers which the children then follow, marking the route with pencil on the map. A number of control markers may also be placed along the trail and these have also to be accurately located on the map. The exercise is particularly useful for developing confidence: it requires the children to perform the skills of solo navigation without the fear of getting lost. It also allows the teacher to cope with fairly large numbers of children at one time. This principle can be modified and used to coach more sophisticated skills, especially terrain memory.

c *Line event*   An alternative means of focusing the beginner's attention on these aspects of map understanding is to mark a route on the map. If the individual follows the route exactly he finds a number of control markers; if he deviates from the route he risks missing the markers. He is not told the position of the markers, nor how many there are, when he starts. Every time he finds a flag he marks its location on his map. This can be a useful way of developing distance judgement and step scales for beginners, especially if the route is confined to paths and major line features, with control markers situated at convenient distances (50m, 100m, 200m etc.) from obvious features, track bends or junctions. This principle is also used for coaching more advanced techniques (see Corridor event p. 76).

During this second stage, the beginners should reinforce their understanding of the basic navigational skills and should be introduced to simple competitive techniques to enable them to come to the essence of orienteering – route choice. Many of the necessary skills can be developed in the practical exercises described above but the most valuable coaching situation occurs after the beginner has completed a course. It is at this point, when the competitor marks the route he followed on his map, that the coach or teacher can begin to focus attention on such techniques as aiming off, the use of collecting and handrail features and the selection and use of good attack points. Hence the post mortem is the most productive period for skills teaching. In a schools context this can be done as a group discussion and maps and routes posted on a notice board can be particularly useful for comparative purposes.

The essence of competitive orienteering is finding the quickest route between the control sites and there are many reasons why this may not be a straight line. The difficulty experienced by beginners is that of identifying possible alternative routes, assessing their relative merits and quickly making a decision, probably on the run. At this point the teacher cannot necessarily provide definitive advice or a fool-proof formula, for navigational decision-making is to some extent a matter of personal ability, fitness and preference. However, the teacher can at least give the beginner some pointers, which may help to inform his decision-making.

The beginner must learn to glean all the vital information quickly for each decision from his map and his observation of the terrain, and the teacher should arrange training exercises to sharpen perception of these matters. A straight line may be the shortest distance between two points but it may well not be the fastest route over the terrain. The orienteer must learn to identify likely obstacles to his progress from his map. For example, he must identify uncrossable features, rivers, fences, private land and cliffs – or slow-progress features – difficult forest, marsh, steep hills or valleys. He must also learn to identify features likely to aid his route choice and progress, handrail features and collecting features and obvious attack points, as discussed earlier.

Some of these things can be taught or coached in theory. In the classroom much can be done using photographic slides of recent competition maps to discuss route-choice possibilities. However, route choice is essentially a personal matter, and can only be done effectively when someone knows his own abilities. The teacher can, at this stage, do something to give individuals this experience. Each orienteer needs to know his relative speed over a whole variety of types of terrain and gradient, both for the purpose of route choice and distance judgement. The teacher should mark a measured distance over a variety of terrains and gradients and each navigator can then time himself over each section and there can be a comparison of relative speeds.

If these measured distances can be marked semi-permanently, so much the better, for they may be checked at regular intervals. Another way of comparing the relative efficiency of two routes is for the teacher to select two features as control sites, offering two broadly similar routes between them. Have the group work in pairs, with one runner taking each route, time them and then have them run the other route for a comparison. Often such semi-competitive exercises can be very revealing for both pupil and the teacher.

STAGE 3: ADVANCED COMPETITIVE TECHNIQUES

The distinction in our scheme for the teacher/coach between Stage 2 (simple competitive skills) and Stage 3 is not clear-cut. As competitors increase in experience they need, in addition to group teaching, individual help and coaching in order to develop slightly more sophisticated techniques. It is the shift in emphasis to the individual that marks the distinction.

The courses the beginner attempts now become more demanding and the navigational problems posed more complex. But the skills remain essentially the same. Clearly, the efficiency of an orienteer's decision-making relates directly to the quality of his experience and a principle of instruction is that the teacher or coach helps the learner to organise his experience. It helps the learner if he can quickly identify the nature of the problem facing him. In orienteering for example, a detour problem could take several forms:

1   Over or round (height v distance).
2   Short difficult terrain v long easy terrain (physical).
3   Short difficult terrain v long easy terrain (technical).

Personal fitness and preference will dictate that no two orienteers meet and solve such problems in an identical way. A feature of good coaching is to help the individual to identify the precise nature of the problem and then relate his own experience to it in order to make the decision.

Any leg on an orienteering course requires the competitor to make a decision about the route to take and then follow that route on the ground.

An important function for the teacher/coach is to help individuals identify weaknesses in the techniques they employ. Frequently the 'right' route is selected but time is wasted in completing it by unnecessary reference to the map. The efficient orienteer probably has a mental check-list of the major features on his route and is able to run the leg without frequent reference to the map. In the school context, as experience increases these skills can be developed by map-memory exercises.

It is not true to say that the distinction between the good orienteer and the bad orienteer is that the former never gets lost and the latter does. But it is more true to suggest that having got lost the bad orienteer spends longer in that state. All competitors get lost at some time but the good navigator identifies his error early, by distance judgement or sensing the fit of the map to the terrain and he applies a systematic technique for relocating his position. This relocation is usually achieved by recalling the terrain that has been crossed and exercises in terrain memory can develop another useful skill in the repertoire of the competitive navigator.

Chapters 5 and 6 deal in detail with the skills and exercises appropriate to this level (contouring, control picking, traffic lights etc.) but perhaps the most important thing the teacher/coach can do for the young people he works with is encourage them to develop a systematic approach to their preparation, both for training and competition. Many minor errors and irritations caused by the stress of competition can be avoided by the competitor who has developed a reliable preparatory procedure and race routine. Security and confidence develop from the familiar and this is very important, especially during the early stages of an orienteering course.

This chapter has attempted to draw a general distinction between the levels of activity involved in introducing others to the sport of orienteering, particularly in schools. The material is based on the joint experience of the authors, gathered over almost a decade of working with beginners and teachers, and we have tried to identify the main categories of orienteering activity in an educational context.

Firstly we believe that the basic skills of navigation and an understanding of maps are fundamental to all forms of field work and outdoor pursuits and that they underpin many educational activities, especially in the area of environmental studies. With this in mind, we feel that there is a strong case for the use of orienteering, preferably in primary schools, as the most practical introduction to the use of maps and navigation.

Secondly, orienteering is a sport and recreational activity which can be enjoyed by a wide range, in terms of age and ability. Our present school games' programmes are being criticised, increasingly, for their bias towards competitive team games. When an individual has a grasp of the simple skills of navigation, orienteering can provide an opportunity for him to compete with himself as well as with other people.

It is at this recreative/competitive level that orienteering has its greatest potential. For example, Walton Chasers, one of the largest orienteering clubs in the U.K., began when Peter Palmer, a passionate disciple of the sport from the first events in this country, became deputy headteacher of Walton Comprehensive School in Stafford, and started to introduce the sport to groups of the students. Before long, parents who were acting as chauffeurs taking their children to events began to walk around the courses themselves, rather than wait in the car park and orienteering became an activity for parents (and dogs) as well as the students. Eventually an open club was formed, based originally on the school, but it has now developed and draws a membership from the whole Stafford area. The success of the club in promoting local orienteering activities, as well as in major national competitions is a tribute to all its members but is particularly a testimonial to Peter Palmer's belief in the value of orienteering as a community recreational activity and the ultimate family sport.

Thirdly, in the educational context, orienteering at its most advanced level provides a serious competitive sport, every bit as demanding physically and mentally as any yet invented by man. It should be recognised that the numbers of students who will actually continue to this stage will probably be small. Many are satisfied to master the simple skills of navigation and enjoy only occasional orienteering events. They do not want, nor will they ever be ready for, more advanced coaching. However, as standards of performance rise and more young people become involved in national and international competition, so the levels of proficiency of the young increase and so does the demand for more sophisticated coaching.

APPENDIX A

The beginner and a typical event

There are a number of questions asked by all beginners to orienteering. Here are a selection of them.

WHAT EQUIPMENT IS REQUIRED?

For the beginner the sport demands very little special clothing or equipment. Any old items of clothing which provide cover for arms and legs and sturdy footwear, such as games boots or light 'fell' boots are ideal for the first event. (Don't be intimidated by 'experts' in light nylon suits and special shoes; you will need a lot of experience before these items will materially improve your performance.) You will also need:

1 A red ball-point or fibre-tip pen to mark your map.
2 A clear plastic bag to use as a map case.
3 A whistle, for use in the most unlikely event of an accident or your becoming totally lost.
4 A compass, although this is not essential for a first event.

ARE ANY SPECIAL SKILLS REQUIRED?

Provided that a beginner selects an appropriate course, designed for 'way-finders' (novices), he needs no special skills or experience beyond the ability to interpret the simple symbols on an orienteering map. A wayfinders' course will normally provide a route using large and obvious features and the navigational problems should be relatively simple. If a beginner spends a few minutes before he sets off studying the legend to check that he understands the symbols on his orienteering map, he should be well able to negotiate the wayfarers' course. Don't be too ambitious in the selection of a course. Start with a short, simple one for it is much better to develop your techniques on the basis of initial success than failure.

WHAT HAPPENS AT A TYPICAL EVENT?

Orienteering competitions are normally staged in wooded areas, so you will probably need to go by car. Travel directions are included in the preliminary information provided by the event organiser, and the organiser usually has the route to the car park sign-posted from the likely approach routes. The easiest way to describe a typical event is to consider what happens, step by step.

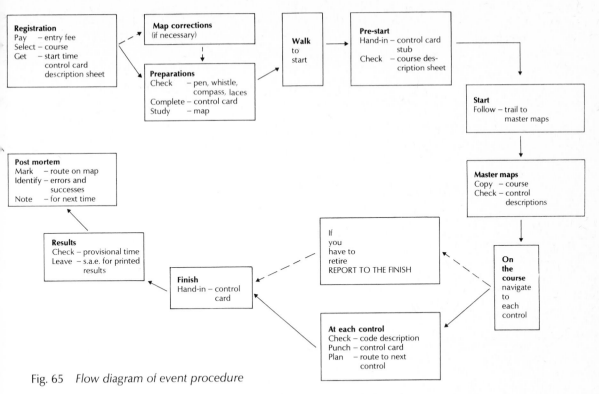

Fig. 65 *Flow diagram of event procedure*

1 Find the event *registration point*, which will normally be near the parking area, either in a tent or the officials may be in a car. A notice in the vicinity will give details of the length and difficulty of each course, although the competitor may already be aware of this from the advance information. The entrant selects a course, pays his entry fee and is given a start time. At registration the competitor should ensure that he has at least 30–40 minutes before he is due off – longer if there is a long walk to the start – in which to complete his preparations and have a good look at the map. Collect your map, control card and a description sheet at the registration.

2 Having registered, the competitor may complete his last-minute pre-parations. For the beginner this would usefully involve checking: that pen, whistle and compass are functioning correctly; that he is ade-quately (but not over-) dressed for the conditions and terrain; that laces are double-tied to prevent their being pulled loose by undergrowth. When satisfied with his personal equipment, the orienteer can turn to specific preparations for the competition. Often, since the map has been produced some weeks before, there have been recent minor changes in the terrain – new forestry work or fencing or a stream diverted. The competitor's map has now to include these details. This he does by copying the *map corrections*, normally on display near to registration. Many competitors also mark arrows indicating north on the magnetic meridian lines and the top of their map, so there is less chance of revers-

ing the map in the forest. Any spare time should be spent studying the map and trying to visualise the main features of the terrain.

The details on both parts of the control card must be completed. The right-hand portion will be given to the official at the pre-start; the other part will be punched by the competitor at each control as evidence of his visit. His card needs to be readily accessible and some map cases have special pockets to hold it. The beginner can content himself by taping the card to the back of the map case. If it is fixed by the top edge only, it can easily be punched at the control. The description sheet can be stuck to the back of the map and another check, to prevent stamping the wrong control, can be provided by copying the control code numbers from the description sheet to the appropriate squares on the control card.

3   With his preparations completed the competitor can move from the assembly area to the race area proper. The walk to the start can be used very profitably to form a general impression of the terrain and the map. Your route to the start area will be marked by streamers. Do not be put off by the feverish antics of élite competitors 'warming up' as they are not competing on your course.

The start procedure varies from one event to another but usually there is a *pre-start*. Here the competitor will be called three minutes before his actual start time, along with all the competitors on other courses who are 'off' at the same time. At the pre-start point the official takes the right-hand portion of the control card. (This is taken to the finish and matched with the part the competitor carries and serves as a safety check for the organiser.) If the description sheet has not been given out during registration, it will be handed to competitors at the pre-start and should be fixed to the back of the map. Normally tapes mark pre-start lines for − 3, − 2 and −1 minute from the start time and groups of competitors move forward to the next tape at every whistle. This gives competitors and officials opportunity to complete all the necessary checks without too much haste.

Eventually it is time to set off. The whistle goes and the beginner, with up to ten others, bursts into the forest, following streamers to the *master maps*.

4   Once there, the competitor checks that he has copied the correct course on to his map. Each master map is identical to his map except that it has a course marked on it:

> He marks the location of the master maps
> He marks each control site
> He marks the finish

This is a critical part of the whole competition, for even a minor error in copying the location of controls could result in many frustrating minutes

– even hours – in the forest. It is well worth the beginner taking extra time to check his working at this stage. Once the master maps have been copied the orienteering proper can begin.

5 When the competitor has navigated to each *control* he should:

   Check the control flag number and description.
   Stamp the appropriate square on the control card with the pin punch at the control.
   Move off from the flag as quickly as possible.

From the final control on each course a marked trail leads to the finish.

6 As the competitor crosses the *finish line* he is timed and his control card collected. This is then checked against the master card codes from the pin punches to see that he has visited the right controls. His overall time is then calculated. A few minutes after finishing, the competitor will see his provisional time posted in the results' ladder. These results will be checked by the organiser after the event and if the competitor leaves money for the postage he normally receives a printed copy of the results a few days after the event.

   If, for some reason, he fails to get as far as the last control and has to retire, he must report to the finish, or at the very least get a message to the finish, giving his name, the course he entered and his start time and explaining that he is safely off the course. If, at the end of a long and hard day, the organisers and other competitors have to search for a competitor they think may be injured on the course, only to find that he went off home or to the pub without reporting to the finish, that person is not likely to be popular!

7 Having reported to the finish, the strenuous part of the day is over. All that remains are the less active aspects of the sport – a picnic perhaps, and watching friends and club mates return, followed by the discussion of routes and errors. Much can be gained from this post mortem and the competitor should mark the route he followed on to his map and make a note of the successes and errors of his day. This information might help improve his route-choice decisions next time.

OBTAINING INFORMATION ABOUT EVENTS

Each copy of *The Orienteer* carries a current fixture list and the name and address of each event organiser. A sheet of preliminary details, giving all the necessary information – venue, date, time, length and nature of courses, entry fees and travel directions – is prepared for each event and is available from the organiser to anyone who sends a stamped and addressed envelope. The most effective way to get information about orienteering events is to join a local club, and B.O.F. will send details of the regional associations and local clubs on receipt of a stamped and addressed envelope at the national office (address at Appendix F).

CAN ANYONE ENTER AN ORIENTEERING EVENT?

In the UK anyone can take part in three competitions on the B.O.F. fixture list (excluding championships), as a guest of the federation, after which he/she must become a member of an affiliated club or region.

APPENDIX B

A selection from the rule of competition

THE COMPETITOR

3.1 Eligibility

A competitor shall not be allowed to take part in more than three events in the national fixture list (except closed events) without becoming a member of the B.O.F. All competitors in Senior Championships shall be individual or family members of the B.O.F. They shall also be either eligible to hold a U.K. passport or have been resident in the U.K. for at least 6 months in the 10 months preceding the event. All competitors in Junior Championships shall be individual, family or group members of the B.O.F.

Officials may refuse entries from competitors they consider unfit to complete the course and those whose intimate knowledge of the terrain would give them an unfair advantage shall be 'non-competitive'.

3.2. Entry

Preliminary information and entry forms may be obtained by sending a stamped addressed envelope to the official whose address is given in the national fixture list. A closing date for entries shall be given for championships.

The following information may be required on entry forms: name and initials, club, class, course preferred, start time, B.O.F. membership number, date of birth, and information for seeding.

3.3. Dress

The form of clothing is optional except that full arm and body protection shall be worn. Competitors shall wear any numbers provided.

3.4. Equipment

Only the map provided shall be used.

A compass, a watch, a writing implement that will not be affected by the weather, and adequate map protection should be carried. These may be required in some events. A whistle shall always be carried, for use in emergencies only (see Section 3.8.).

3.5. Respect for property and the public
Nothing shall be done to prejudice the goodwill of landowners or of their tenants or agents. Competitors shall not deliberately enter out-of-bounds areas. If they find they have done so inadvertently they shall leave the areas without delay. Any competitor whose right to be in an area is challenged shall stop, explain his presence, comply with any reasonable request (even if this means abandoning the race) and inform the challenger of the location of the nearest responsible official. On leaving the race, the competitor shall give an account of the occurrence to the finish official or the organiser.

When out-of-bounds areas are given as map corrections, competitors shall mark them accurately on their maps. All obviously private and enclosed properties such as gardens are out-of-bounds.

No attempt shall be made to cross boundaries marked on the map as uncrossable, except where a crossing place is indicated.

Care shall be taken to avoid doing any damage. Any damage done or seen to have been done shall be reported to a responsible official. Competitors shall comply with all landowners' requests brought to their notice.

Respect and consideration shall be shown to all members of the public in or near the competition area. All competitors shall comply with the country code. Smoking is prohibited in the competition area. Dogs shall not be brought into the area without permission. No litter shall be left. It is forbidden to set foot on growing crops or newly sown land. To avoid disturbing farm animals competitors shall walk if necessary.

3.6. Abandoning the race and leaving the course
Every competitor who has started the competition shall hand in his control card to the finish official, whether he has finished the course or not. A competitor who has lost his control card shall report the fact to the finish official. Only under conditions of extreme duress is a competitor excused from these duties.

3.7. Fair Play
Contests in orienteering shall be conducted in the spirit of fairness and good fellowship. Participants shall not seek to obtain unfair advantages over their fellow competitors. Any search for the competition course or inspection of the area before the race is prohibited.

All competitors shall race independently, except when they are entered as a pair or group. It is not allowed for one competitor to follow another deliberately. Shouting and calling are prohibited. Competitors shall not deliberately give away the position of controls. Every competitor shall follow any reasonable instructions of any race official; in particular he shall show his card to a control official on request.

Competitors who have finished the race or retired shall not assist others or influence the progress of the contest in any way. They are not entitled to re-enter the competition area until the race is ended, and may be required to hand in their maps until the last competitor has started.

3.8. Safety and emergencies

The international distress signal is six blasts on the whistle (or 6 shouts or flashes of a torch), then a pause before repeating the pattern. On hearing this or finding a casualty, a competitor shall give help. Normally one person should mark the casualty's position on his map and seek medical help as quickly as possible usually through a responsible official. Another person should stay with the casualty and keep him warm and comfortable.

A young or inexperienced orienteer who is lost and asks for help should be shown his position on the map, and his name noted and reported to the finish official.

Competitors shall not enter for courses they cannot reasonably expect to complete. Newcomers to the sport shall take part in the easiest course except with permission of a responsible official.

3.9. Competitor's Risk

Competitors take part in orienteering events at their own risk.

CONTROL TERMINOLOGY

Task of the control description

The purpose of the control description is to clarify the picture given by the map of the control site. The control description must define the control site as precisely and as briefly as possible.

5.1. Lay out of the control description

1. Number of the control, e.g. 5.
2. Control symbol in brackets, e.g. 5 (DP).
3. Actual description of the site, e.g. 5 (DP) Hill, W foot.
4. Other relevant information, e.g. Barbed wire, E of the control.

5.2. Example of a control description list

M43 10·2kms. Course closes 14.30hrs.
1. (CE) Knoll (1·5m).
2. (DP) Hill W foot. Barbed wire W of control.
3. (GL) Niche.
Follow marked route 200m.
4. (K) Boulder (3 × 2 × 1·5m) E side.
5. (L) Marsh (⌀ 6m) NW edge.
Follow marked route to finish 300m.

5.3. Clarification of terms

Knoll: small hill, height 1–5m.

Hill: height 5–20m.
Big Hill: height more than 20m.
Depression: natural hollow.
Saddle: low point on ridge between two summits.
Pass: passage through higher ground.
Terrace: level area on a slope.
Spur: as at the end of a ridge.
Rib: narrow sloping spur with one side sharp and almost vertical.
Re-entrant: valley; inverted spur (all sizes).
Gully: very narrow re-entrant; ravine.
Crag: insurmountable rocky slope.
Pond: pit or depression filled with water.
River: natural water course, more than 5m broad.
Stream: natural water course, less than 5m broad.
Ditch: artificial water course, sometimes dry.
Marsh: marshy ground, deeper than 30cms.
Open marsh: marsh with no trees growing on it.
Uncrossable marsh: dangerous or unpleasant to cross.
Outcrop: small crag not exceeding 5m in height.
Shallow marsh: marshy ground, less than 30cms thick.
Firm Ground: non-marshy area in marshy area.
Field: regularly cultivated area.
Copse: wooded area in a field or other open area.
Meadow: pasture; area growing grass either sown or natural.
Clearing: area with no trees within the forest; not a felled area.
Felled area: area where trees have been felled for timber extraction.
Plantation: young forest with trees up to about 2m high.
Thicket: area of forest where the undergrowth or trees are so dense
    that it is difficult to pass.
Vegetation Boundary: boundary between different types of vegetation.
Bare rock: area of surface rock, usually open.
Rocky knoll: knoll made of bare rock, 1–5m high.
Rocky hill: hill of bare rock more than 5m high.
Boulder: block of stone generally greater than 1·5m high.
Boulder field: area covered fairly evenly with boulders or rocks.
Sandy area: area covered with sand.
Road: suitable for cars.
Narrow road: single lane road suitable for cars, usually surfaced.
Track: unsurfaced track suitable for a cart or tractor.
Footpath: large and small.
Foot bridge: bridge for pedestrians.
Building: dwelling-house or factory building.
Hut: shed, barn, outhouse etc.
Foundation: intact foundation.

Ruin: derelict building.
Boundary: wall, fence, hedge, earthbank.
Boundary stone: prominent boundary marker.
Ride: clearly visible linear gap in the forest; firebreak.
Pit: working where sand, gravel, clay or mud has been removed, and
    which cannot be described with normal symbols because of shape.
Mineshaft: generally a small quarry or shaft.
Charcoal burning ground: remains of former charcoal burning area.

5.4. Terms for control sites

Edge: site on the border of an area (e.g. Marsh, E edge), or on the border of, as
    opposed to 'in' a pit (Gravel pit, W edge).
Corner: where the edge of the feature, turns through an angle of 45–165°
    (Field, E corner).
Tip: where the edge of the feature turns through an angle less than 45°
    (Marsh, N tip).
Bend: site actually at the bend shown by the linear symbol on the map (Path
    bend).
Part: site in the middle of a distinct section of an area. The marker should be
    visible from a distance of at least half the radius of the part viewed from
    any direction (Marsh, W part).
Side: site beside a feature which rises above the surface of the earth (i.e. a
    boulder, building, ruin etc.) e.g. Boulder, W side.
Foot: site on the foot line of a contour feature where the slope becomes
    horizontal (Hill, E foot).
End: at the end of a linear feature (ride end) or at some other distinct terminal
    point (Cliff foot, E end).
Junction: where linear features cross (Path ride crossing).
Diameters: ∅ distance across.

5.5. Other requirements

5.5.1. The list of control descriptions shall state the class for which it is
    intended and the length of the course.

5.5.2. The control marker shall be hung in the middle of the feature unless the
    description indicates otherwise.

5.5.3. The size of the feature shall be given in the description if it is not
    apparent from the map and is not a piece of general knowledge. Thus
    the size of a boulder, boundary stone, marsh smaller than 15m or small
    cliff shall be indicated, whereas the size of a spring, charcoal pit or ruin
    does not need to be given.

5.5.4. The list of control descriptions shall include mention of any marked
    route on the course, and state their lengths. A description for the Start
    and Finish is not given if there are marked routes to them.

5.5.5. When control descriptions are produced in several languages, each
    list shall contain control numbers and control symbols.

5.5.6. The marker shall be clearly visible immediately on reaching the point described in the control description.

5.5.7. Where three dimensions are given the height shall be given last, e.g. (5 × 4 × 3m high).

5.5.8. One of a group (more than 2) of features is indicated by the term 'most' e.g. westernmost.

APPENDIX C

Recommended course lengths and winning times

Class	Time (minutes)	Possible length (km)
Under 15	35	2–4
Under 19	50	4–7
Under 35	65	8–12
Under 50	50	6–8
Over 50	50	4–7

Ladies' courses should be 10–15% less and remember that although the junior winner may take 35 minutes those at the tail-end are likely to be out for 2 hours! Juniors should not be expected to run full-out for longer than 30–35 minutes.

APPENDIX D

Check list for organising a small event

A major orienteering competition requires an elaborate organisation and an army of helpers but, assuming a map is available, a small competition for club or school is fairly straightforward and could be handled by one person if necessary. The following notes are intended to provide a check list for the organiser of a small-scale event. They are not exhaustive and those requiring further information should refer to the appropriate B.O.F. publications.

BEFORE THE EVENT

1   Get permission for access to the land.
2   Consider insurance (only events appearing on the B.O.F. official fixture list are covered by the insurance policy of the Federation. Some L.E.A.s have an insurance policy covering their teachers and school groups).
3   Plan courses.
4   Prepare:

> The map – amendments, corrections and out-of-bounds areas.
> Master maps.
> Control description sheets.
> Control cards.
> Signs and notices.
> Start lists.
> Control flags and punches.

5   Assemble equipment for:

> Registration – maps, description sheets, control cards, start lists.
> Start – box for stubs, whistle, tapes.
> Master maps – notices and map boards.
> Control flags – check tapes.
> Finish – watch, boxes for control cards and tapes.
> Results – string and stapling machine.
> General – pens, scissors, cellotape, staples etc.

(If you are going to make a habit of organising events it is probably a good idea to keep an equipment box for some of these items.)

ON THE DAY

Before the start

1   Put out the controls (make sure plenty of time is allowed).
2   Set up registration.
3   Put out the master maps.
4   Put out tapes to master maps and finish.
5   Set off competitors.

During the event

1   Prepare string for provisional results.
2   Begin working out results for early starters.

After the event

1 Check that all competitors have returned.

2 Collect control flags.

3 Collect all tapes, markers, signs and litter (the sport depends upon the goodwill of landowners. Ensure that nothing is done to jeopardise this).

4 Produce final results.

The list is not really as daunting as it looks. It is quite possible to run a perfectly successful competition for up to 50 people single-handed. It does get more difficult if a high proportion of those taking part are beginners and require individual help.

APPENDIX E

Equipment

The following publications are published by and available from the B.O.F.
Rules of Competition.
Orienteering Techniques.
Course Planning.
Manual for Instructors.
Map Making for Orienteers.
Map Symbol Sheet – Letraset

GENERAL

Orienteering, John Disley, Faber, 1967.
Know the Game – Orienteering, J. D. Watson, E.P. Publishing Ltd, 1973.
Discovering Orienteering, Tony Walker, Shire Publications, 1972.
Orienteering – An Aid to Training, Capt. R. Chapman, Cadet Supply Department, 1968.

INTRODUCTORY

Your Way with Map and Compass, John Disley, Blond Educational, 1972.
Starting from Maps, Schools Council Environmental Studies Project, Hart-Davies, 1972 (concerned with use of maps in primary schools).

Films and Slides

Thomas – the Orienteer. Colour, sound, 16mm, 20 minutes. Hire from Rank

Film Library. Thomas is a young lad at school, who takes up orienteering as his main interest. He joins a club and we see him learning the theory and practice of solving orienteering problems.

Vi Orienterar. Basic instructional slide set (59 slides), suitable for introducing the sport to novices. Hire from the B.O.F. Lea Green, Matlock, Derbyshire DE4 5GJ.

Orienteering Techniques. Advanced Instructional Slide Set (59 slides) for competent orienteers. Hire from B.O.F., Lea Green, Matlock, Derbyshire DE4 5GJ.

The School Goes Orienteering. Colour, sound, 16mm, 30 minutes. Hire from Jordanhill College, Glasgow, Scotland, Audio-Visual Media Department. The film covers the preparation and training of a school team to improve their techniques and ends with the team winning the novice class at a district schools event.

A selection of films on orienteering is available from the B.O.F., Lea Green, Matlock, Derbyshire, DE4 5GJ.

Equipment Suppliers

Compasses, control markers, control punches, control cards etc. from Silva Compasses (London) Ltd, 76 Broad Street, Teddington, Middlesex.
Orienteering suits, shoes and other clothing from: The Sweat Shop, 76 Broad Street, Teddington, Middlesex and Jo Royle, High Peak Outdoor Centre, 22 High Street, Buxton, Derbyshire.

Equipment for the Teacher/Leader

MAPS

The most important item of equipment for any orienteer is a map. B.O.F. are trying to encourage orienteering clubs to produce maps which can be used by clubs, schools or groups for training purposes. A teacher should contact his local club or region (addresses from the B.O.F.) and enquire if any such maps are available in his area. If this fails the 6in and 25in O.S. series can be used to introduce beginners to the basic skills. The maps can be easily 'doctored' and updated (see Chapter 8) and then photocopied (remember the O.S. royalty!).

COMPASS

Orienteers generally use one of the protractor-type compasses supplied by the firms already listed in Appendix E. There is no way a teacher leader can ultimately avoid the expense of providing compasses but much basic teaching can be done with the map alone. Some L.E.A.s and youth organisations have a stock of compasses that they are prepared to loan to schools or groups.

CONTROL MARKERS

It is possible to buy commercially produced markers but initially these may be improvised using painted plastic bottles, or large jam tins from the school kitchen. They are, however, cumbersome to carry.

It is not difficult to make B.O.F. standard control markers from industrial nylon and fencing wire. The dimensions are given in Fig. 66.

Punches and stamps are certainly not essential equipment at the outset, for control markers can contain a number and a code. Beginners can be told the number of the flag and asked to write the code on the control card. If preferred, coloured pencils or spirit-based marker pens could be hung from the markers for the competitors to write the code. This provides a further check and competitors need not then carry pencils.

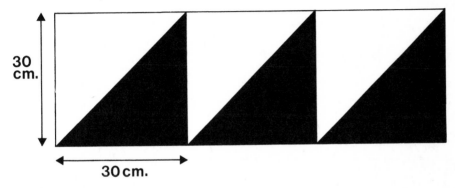

Fig. 66   *Construction of control marker*

APPENDIX F

The British Orienteering Federation

NATIONAL OFFICE

Lea Green,
Nr Matlock,
Derbyshire DE4 5GJ. Telephone: Dethick (062984) 561.

REGIONAL ASSOCIATIONS AND CLUBS

Enquiries concerning regional associations and orienteering clubs should be sent to the national office and current information will be provided (enclose a stamped and addressed envelope).

Structure and Organisation

The basic structure of the B.O.F., which also reflects the lines of authority within the sport, is very simple. The Council carries responsibility for the national administration of the sport whilst the regional associations (12 in all), work closely with local clubs to administer the sport within their respective regions.

The Council committees each have a specialised field of activity and formulate proposals which are submitted for discussion first by regional committees and then by the council. The following fields of responsibility are covered by the committees:

Administration and finance.
Mapping.
International activities.
Training and development.
Competitions.
Fixtures.
Publications (includes translations).
Schools and juniors.
Ski-orienteering.

The full Council consists of the chairman, vice-chairman, secretary, treasurer and representatives of regions. The professional officer, chairmen of the committees and elected officers with special responsibilities (fixtures secretary, statistician and editors of our magazine *The Orienteer* and newsletter *Stop Press*) also attend council meetings.

Our professional officer is directly responsible to the council for all his activities and his broad areas of interest are the smooth functioning of administration, coordination of the activities of all committees and general development of the sport. Every person concerned with the administration of our sport is an active orienteer and is therefore very much aware of what is going on right down to the grass roots.

The National Badge Scheme

Badges are awarded on the results of national events (those which appear in capitals in the fixture list). The scheme is open to all orienteers (except wayfinders) who have competed on their own and reached the required standard in three events.

Gold   Better than the average of the first three competitors' times plus 25%.
Silver   Better than the average of the first three competitors' times plus 50%.
Bronze   Better than the average of the first three competitors' times plus 100%.
Iron   Successful completion of the course.

These standards now apply to all classes with the exception of *all* B classes, where silver standard becomes plus 25% and bronze plus 50%.

Should there be fewer than 20 competitors in a class the average of the first two only is taken. If there are fewer than 10, the winner's time alone is used for the calculation of the standards. At the controller's discretion the badge scheme may not apply for small classes if no competitor achieves a satisfactory time.

Initially competitors are restricted to obtaining their badges in their own class. But holders of a boy's/girl's gold award may compete in a junior class and likewise holders of a junior gold may compete in intermediate classes and those with an intermediate gold may compete in senior classes. The present age limits of the classes mean that there is a time limit of three years for obtaining a badge; this will also apply in senior classes.

If a current gold standard competitor wishes to compete in a B class for personal reasons, his time shall not be included in calculations for determining the badge standards in that class.

To apply for a badge, give the following information:

1   Your name and the class in which you are claiming a badge. If this is not your age class, please give details of your previous gold award.

2   The names and dates of the events concerned.

3   Your place and time in each event.

B.O.F. Coaching Award Scheme

In 1973 B.O.F. introduced a Coaching Award Scheme. The general details follow. For further information write to the national office or your regional secretary.

Structure

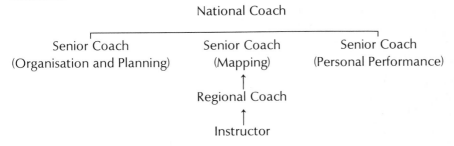

Courses
Throughout the year the 12 regions of the Federation hold instructional courses for the 'Instructor' grade. In addition the Federation organises one week or weekend courses at central venues in Great Britain for those applicants who may have difficulty in attending a local regional course at a given time.

Restriction of awards

There will be no restriction on people attending courses leading to awards or entering the assessment examination (provided they satisfy the conditions of entry) but an award will only be issued if the candidate is a current member of the British Orienteering Federation.

A coaching award qualification will be valid for two years. At the end of this period the holder must apply for re-assessment. The re-assessment will be a simple administrative exercise to ensure that the holder is keeping up to date with advances in the sport and that he is actively utilising his qualification.

Conditions of entry and examination

INSTRUCTOR CERTIFICATE
Conditions of entry. A candidate must:
(a) be over 18 years of age;
(b) have attended an approved instructors' course (can attend from age of 16) and have studied and be conversant with the instructor's manual;
(c) have successfully completed the course appropriate to his/her age group in at least three 'club standard' competitions organised under B.O.F. rules during the preceding twelve months;
(d) have assisted in the organisation and instruction for two introductory courses or come and try it events;
(e) pay an entry fee of £1.

Examination will take the form of three separate units which could conceivably be conducted consecutively on the same day.

a **Practical Teaching.** The candidate must demonstrate the ability to coach the skills of orienteering to a group of at least four students. He/she will be required to prepare and conduct a short coaching session on a topic named by the assessor. In order to provide genuine beginners rather than 'stooges' for the candidates to teach, it is suggested that candidates could instruct in the named topic at an introductory course advertised in the normal way. If the candidate is a student teacher he could be assessed whilst on teaching practice.

b **Practical Event Organisation.** A qualified controller will attend at a small scale event organised by the candidate to ensure that all details are in order for this standard of competition. Particular attention will be paid to the candidate's ability to plan suitable courses and to place controls accurately at the points marked on the master maps.

c **Written and Oral Examination.** A wide basic knowledge of orienteering is expected. Candidates must demonstrate knowledge of:
  i history of the sport
  ii structure and function of B.O.F.
  iii B.O.F. rules of orienteering
  iv elementary surveying and map preparation
  v organisation of a small cross country event and other types of competition (score, street, line, point, etc.)
  vi training aids and training exercises
  vii safety and elementary first aid
  viii country code.

REGIONAL COACH CERTIFICATE

Conditions of entry. A candidate must hold a current Instructor's Certificate.

Examination. No examination, as such, will be organised for this grade. Candidates must supply the Coaching and Training Sub-Committee with evidence to prove that he/she:

(a) is a Grade II Controller.

(b) is of current (i.e. within previous 12 months) silver badge standard.

(c) has drawn an orienteering map (black and white or coloured) and has taken an active part in the field surveying for an orienteering map.

Candidates will pay an entry fee of 40p.

SENIOR COACH CERTIFICATE

Conditions of Entry. A candidate must:

(a) be over 21 years of age;

(b) have attended an approved national course in their chosen speciality (can attend from 18 upwards) and have studied and be conversant with the appropriate manuals.

(c) be a holder of a current Instructor's Certificate;

(d) pay an entry fee of £2.

There will be 3 types of Senior Coach – Organisation and Planning, Personal Performance, Mapping.

Organisation and Planning

(a) The candidate will be expected to be a Grade I Controller.

(b) The candidate will be expected to have:

    i acted as the Organiser of a Federation event of at least Badge standard.

    ii acted as the Planner of a Federation event of at least Badge standard.

A critical assessment of all aspects of these competitions will be made prior and subsequent to the events as well as during the day of the competition. Particular attention will be paid to the arrangements for the Start, Finish and Results as well as the suitability of all the courses.

Personal Performance

(a) The candidate will be expected to have achieved a Gold standard in his/her age group.

(b) A detailed knowledge will be required of:

    i the different techniques e.g. coarse orienteering, fine orienteering, traffic lights, route choice etc., their use in varying types of terrain and practice and theoretical exercises involving these techniques.

    ii personal fitness training with particular reference to the needs of the sport. The candidates will be expected to be fully acquainted with the various methods of training including Fartlek, interval, long distance, tempo and speed and to be able to prepare a suitable training programme for all types of competitor.

    iii the psychology of training, physiology, training aids and diet.

Mapping

(a) The candidate will be expected to have produced or coordinated the production of an orienteering map of a high standard. The assessor will visit the area covered by the map and particular attention will be paid to the suitability of the scale, selection of orienteering detail, and the accuracy and uniformity of the map.

(b) A detailed knowledge will be required of: field survey methods, interpretation of air photographs, map compilation, drawing methods. Also an understanding of the advantages and limitations of the use of photogrammetry and of the methods and requirements of the printer.

Examination for all types of Senior Coach will be of the following format.

(a) The candidate will be required to act as a member of staff on a National course on his chosen speciality of at least two days' duration. A critical assessment will be made of the candidate's ability during this period.

(b) A written and oral paper of two hours' duration on the candidates chosen speciality.

Assessment

Candidates who feel they satisfy the Conditions of Entry should apply for assessment. Assessment for the Instructor's Certificate will be conducted on a regional basis as and when the need arises. In addition the British Orienteering Federation will hold one or two national assessment weekends at a central venue for those candidates who are unable to attend a regional assessment.

Duke of Edinburgh's Award Scheme

ORIENTEERING
The Duke of Edinburgh's Award Scheme

Section: Interest (boys and girls)

This programme is for *guidance* and is *not* to be taken as a rigid syllabus to be followed.

Emphasis is laid on *regular* participation and as much improvement as possible in the period – but assessment should *not* be solely on standard of skill attained.

Participants should be members of either a school club or an official Orienteering club.

At all levels candidates should keep a log-book giving details of instruction received; books read and details of *all* events competed in, including a map with the course, and course post-mortem giving brief factual and critical details of their route together with results. More advanced participants could also comment on the course itself – interest and difficulty etc.

For Beginners

1 Demonstrate the use of a Silva compass; orientate a map and take correct bearing.
2 Understand IOF symbols in common use.
3 Knowledge of 1:20,000 and 1:10,000 map scales and how far on the ground a set length on the map would be. (In metres or paces taken).
4 Be able to read a map so as to describe a route.
5 Basic knowledge of the meaning of contours.
6 Be able to copy accurately a course from a master map.
7 Understand Rules of Competition relating to candidate in competition, e.g. use of emergency whistle.
8 Basic knowledge of common orienteering control terminology.
9 To have attempted at least 8 courses and achieved BOF Iron standard (or equivalent in club events).
10 Keep a log-book.

For participants with some knowledge before starting e.g. a year's experience
All items 1–10
11 Understand a wider range of IOF symbols.

12 Use of accurate pace judgement.
13 More detailed knowledge of contours including recognition of contour features and judging of gradient.
14 Route choice and points to be considered.
15 Understanding basic techniques such as use of attack points, aiming off, catching features, handrails etc.
16 To help, if possible, with organisation of a local event.
17 To have achieved BOF Bronze standard in their own age group.
18 Have some knowledge of different types of event organised – cross country, score, relays etc.

For participants with considerable knowledge (at least 2 years' experience)
All items 1–18
19 Knowledge of training, both physical and technical, that can be undertaken to improve one's standard.
20 Some knowledge of BOF Organisation, at club, regional and national level.
21 Help plan or organise a simple event.
22 Plan a course for own age group on a map provided by the assessor – showing knowledge of essentials of a good course.
23 To have achieved BOF Silver standard for their own age group.

Section: Physical Activities (boys and girls)
GOLD   30 points to be gained
To be awarded as follows:

BOYS

B.O.F. Gold standard achieved	24
Silver	18
Bronze	12
For completing a course at the British Junior Championships	3
For completing courses at	
Regional Championships	2
Badge Events and Schools Championships	2
Other Events	1

GIRLS

B.O.F. Gold Standard achieved	18
Silver	14
Bronze	8
For completing a course at	
British Junior Championships	4
Regional Championships	3
Badge and School Championships	2
Other Events	1

SILVER   24 points to be gained

BOYS only

B.O.F. Gold	16
Silver	12
Bronze	8
For completing courses	as for Gold

BRONZE   18 points to be gained

BOYS only

B.O.F. Gold	10
Silver	8
Bronze	6
For completing courses	as for Gold

At all standards they must have competed in a minimum of 6 events. They should be members of an orienteering club.

Candidates will be expected to be reasonably knowledgeable about all the above aspects of the sport, and to be able to answer straightforward questions, not only about competing, but also about the organisation of an event.

All applications for purposes of assessment in the Fitness Section of the Duke of Edinburgh's Award Scheme should be addressed to:

The National Statistician,
Mrs J. Buckley,
British Orienteering Federation,
5 Cherry Tree Avenue, Belper, Derbyshire.

Index